an airing of **dirty laundry**

WILLIAM (BILL) CUTTANCE

All correspondence to the author:
Email: bcuttan@msn.com

First Printed 2021

ISBN: 978-0-6452836-0-0

Proudly produced by

TheBookStudio
www.thebookstudio.com.au

DEDICATED TO MY SONS

Who have had to put up with a lot!

Author's Note

This is a series of fictionalised tales based on happenings during my 70 odd years tenure in the finance world. They are set in the 1970/80s when I was in the thick of it and in a small make-believe entity I have adopted for the purpose, the 'Australian Banking Company' (ABC Bank).

Because of the commodity they deal in, Banks possess their own unique culture. They are notoriously secretive, bound by longstanding banking law not to disclose the financial dealings of customers. They also zealously guard their reputation against any scandal to ensure their standing as sound, trust-worthy safe-keepers of money is never jeopardised. So, it is a deliberate ploy on their part "to tell 'em nuthin" on the basis that "if they don't know, they can't rock the boat."

Banks aggressively pursue profit and because of their constant hard-ball approach, banker/customer relationships are not always harmonious. When disputes arise, Banks always claim the high ground, never conceding error. They fight hard and their customers have a difficult time gaining the upper hand. Rarely, does this intransience meet with any serious scrutiny.

On the other side of the banking counter, it is little different. Bank customers also jealously guard their privacy and hold their seamy secrets tight.

We have scant inkling of what goes on.

Against that background, I have lifted the lid a little to give a glimpse inside this secretive world and into the lives of those within it. I hope you enjoy the read and that perhaps when you next visit your bank, you might look at the people behind the counter and wonder whether any are hiding a guilty secret behind a smiling, poker face.

Bill Cuttance

The Exclusion of Women (1970/1980s)

When reading these tales, one may be struck by the glaring absence of women exercising power.

In those times, membership of Bank boards and access to senior ranks were the exclusive preserve of men. There were no women branch managers, or even tellers for that matter. The most senior women employed were the "head girls" in Administrative typing pools and records sections or as secretaries to the big men.

It was a male dominated society. There were women working in traditional roles such as nurses and teachers and in lesser status positions elsewhere. Many men, particular older ones, still held the traditional view that a woman's place was in the home looking after the house and the kids. It was, in fact, only a few years earlier that the "marriage bar" was lifted, a legislative requirement that when a woman in the public service married, she had to give up her job and leave.

Young men too universally perceived women as lesser creatures. Typically, for example, it was well known that "chicks couldn't surf". Confirmation of this "truth" was ventilated in Kathy Lette and Gabrielle Carey's 1979 coming of age novel '*Puberty Blues*'. The story centres around Wanda Beach in Sydney's Sutherland shire and a group of teenagers, their casual sex, alcohol and drugs and highlights the subservient role of the young women.

As Kathy Lette commented following the subsequent TV series, "It brought back in a raw rush what it was like to be treated as little more than life support to a pair of breasts. We surfie girls were runners up in the human race. We were not allowed to ride surfboards. Our only role was to fetch the boys' chiko rolls for lunch, massage their egos and mind the towels."

(Kathy Lette (2013) "Channel 10 Interview – Puberty Blues" @ http://10Play.com.au)

This is an incisive reminder of what the world was like even for young women at that time.

It was no wonder that deprived of a more varied life many women having seen the kids off to school, finished their household chores, said to themselves in utter frustration, "is this all there is?" In such situations, the popular saying immortalised in Australian culture at that time was "have a nice cuppa, a Bex and a good lie down!" ('Bex' was a popular analgesic in powder form designed for ailments such as headache and fever. However, it contained codeine and possessed relaxing qualities. Whilst addictive, it was popular among women, and we can see why.)

This era though did see the first cracks in the wall keeping women out. Singer Helen Reddy with her single *'I am Woman'* was encouraging women to throw away their aprons and stand up for themselves. At the same time, Germaine Greer and other feminist writers were setting the cat amongst the pigeons and senior management in the business world was slowly coming to realise the need to open-up employment doors to women.

Banks were very slowly allowing women into junior lending, accounting and administrative roles. A few women tellers started to appear on branch counters.

Over the years since, there has been gradual general improvement across the board with women now regularly filling powerful positions in the commercial hierarchy. However, there remains a long way to go especially in respect to the never-ending harassment and violence and parity in employment remuneration. The struggle to overcome these and other issues continues.

It needs to be recognised then when reading these stories that in the era in question, chauvinism was very much alive and well!

Contents

BLOODY BANKERS!

The rapacious reputation of banks disclosed in recent times
has tarnished their image and those who work for them.
So, as a former banker, I am disappointed that...

My colleagues and I are no longer held in the esteem we once were.

The consensus is
we can't be trusted.

We are rude and arrogant.

We are rogues.

We charge people exorbitant fees
even when drawing out their own money.

When you go for a loan cap in hand,
we put you through the third degree.
We try to find reasons why we cannot give it to you.
And
when we do finally agree,
we make you feel like we are doing you a favour.

Surely, we cannot be that bad!
Are we?

So...
I sought the view of Cynthia
a close forthright friend
a highly qualified legal identity.

But
who runs her own escort agency?

"Yes", she said, "I have known a few of your colleagues.
They are mostly up themselves.
Self-opiniated RIMS – Big wheels but lacking the essential guts.
Mostly poorly educated with little sophistication.
They talk big but about themselves and the bloody bank.
Their main interests are beer, football, and meat pies.
They have little interest in the finer things of life;
classical music, ballet, opera, or good wine.
I don't think they have ever read a good book.
If I ever talk about someone like Solzhenitsyn
they ask, "Who does he play for?"
Or, they say
"Don't know him! With that name he must be a soccer player."
Ye Gods and little fishes !!!!!!!!
They have money but are mean and stingy.
They have long pockets and want a lot for nothing.
Getting down to the nitty gritty,
they generally have small appendages.
And worse still
they have no idea how to turn my key.
When put to the test,
their performance is mediocre to say the least.
Invariably, wham, bang, thank you, Maam!
In my view, a very deluded lot."

"Gee Cynthia" I said, "that is terrible.
Are we all like that?"

Putting her arm around my waist and pulling me close,
she looked up smilingly and said,
"Of course not, Darling Man, there are exceptions!!!!!"

THE AUSTRALIAN BANKING COMPANY

(The ABC Bank - *A Fictional Entity*)

The ABC Bank was one of the country's smallest Banks. It had a network of nearly 300 branches distributed across every state and territory but predominantly on the eastern seaboard. Its Head Office was situated at Circular Quay in Sydney.

It provided a full range of banking services in both consumer and corporate fields and competed aggressively in the market until it was taken over by one of the big banks in the late 1980s.

About a third of its business was held in New South Wales and which was managed and administered by a separate group established for this purpose.

Subject to the overview by Head Office, control was vested in a State Manager and an executive group of a Deputy State Manager and four Group Leaders. Three of the latter each controlled a section of the state's lending according to geographical location (designated Northern, Western and Southern Divisions). A fourth Group Leader supervised general administrative matters, branch and retail operations.

PHILLIP FALLON

A Good Man

His colleagues initially called him Phil but more often "Philly". Some years earlier there had been a champion racehorse filly called Flight who captured the public's admiration for her gameness and winning ways. Some wag recalled this and in the light of the constant "Philly" and his readiness "to have a go" decided to declare Phillip Fallon "Flite". It stuck and he was well known throughout the Bank's service by this pseudonym.

Flite was the junior among the executive Group Leaders. He was not in the conservative banker mould, a thinker outside the square and sometimes dissident. He held a commerce degree from the University of New South Wales and was the only senior executive manager with tertiary education. He was studying for his Masters in "Forensic Accounting" at night at the University of Sydney.

He had been brought up on the wrong side of the tracks, his father dying in a pub brawl when he was 10. His mother struggled financially and Flite had learned at a young age the value of money. After he left school, he attended university by day and worked in a soap factory at night to earn enough to live on. It was tough going. After graduating, he joined the Bank and worked in the Treasury and Accounting Department. He showed early that he was destined for higher things and with his sound judgment and no-nonsense approach he progressed rapidly through the ranks. When promoted to Group Leader within the NSW Administration, he was the youngest to have ever attained this status.

He was happily married with twin daughters who were keen pony club members. For their sake, Flite had bought a home with stables on acreage close to Camden on Sydney's southern edge.

His prime Bank responsibility was the state's branch operations. He performed well and the State Manager, Simon Sinclair, relied on him heavily as his trouble shooter to overcome the inevitable challenges that arose. He was perceived by staff as a good decent man.

OTHERS WHO FIGURE PROMINENTLY

Simon Sinclair – State Manager NSW
Les Ferguson – Deputy State Manager NSW
Norman MacLeod – Group Leader, Southern Division
Bryn O'Toole – Bank Friend of Phillip Fallon
Sandy Montagu – Manager, Coolong (Coolong Plains)
Charles Cooper DFC. DSO. – Manager, Ashley Grove
Edward J. (Teddy) Chomley – Assistant Manager Ashley Grove
Celeste (Rodriquese) deLiano
Bill Hansen – Manager, Tempe
Arthur Smythe-Parker – Collection Agent
Albert Wright – Internal Auditor
Erik Nielsen – Senior Loans Manager – Southern Division
Therese Briden – Human Resources Officer
Rick Ryan – Teller
Sue Carney – Staff and Payroll Officer
Tony Rossi – Home Loans Officer – Southern Division
Tom Perkins – Head Messenger
Timothy Flattery – Messenger
Heidi Gustafson – Switch Board
The Papas family – Georgi, Paulos, Nic, Mimi and Demetios
The Calabrians – Bruno, Joe, Lennie
Ivan Katanov - A KGB Man
Lindsay Kelly – Rails Bookmaker
Tony Parkes – His Assistant

None of these people are real. Any resemblance to individuals past or present is coincidental.

SUE CARNEY

Who became a Union Advocate

Sue was the NSW Admin's personnel clerk responsible for staff records and most importantly, the payroll.

Staff salaries were paid to their respective accounts every second Thursday by an external payroll firm.

On the Tuesday before payday, Sue completed a schedule setting out the changes to the previous pay. On completion, it was checked by the Chief Clerk and after authorisation by the State Manager, it was couriered with the Bank's cheque to the payroll firm for processing.

The Admin's internal auditor, Albert Wright was required to undertake periodic checks to ensure that everything was in order.

Sue was in her late thirties, divorced, unhappy and bitter following her marital break-up. She was aggressive and constantly critical of fellow staff and management. She had a couple of women friends but mostly kept to herself.

Whilst she herself was competent, her immediate boss, Chief Clerk, Jimmy Harper, was a ditherer. He had been promoted to NSW Admin from a Head Office department where he had filled a similar role but not very well. The other department had "pushed him upstairs" to get rid of him. He had difficulty in making decisions and passed over to Sue as many onerous responsibilities as he could.

When the Chief Clerk position had become vacant, Sue expected to get the job. When she didn't, she was disappointed and disillusioned. She grew angry inside and further alienated by constantly holding Jimmy's hand and doing the things he should be doing.

She kept telling herself, "I am doing the job but not getting paid for it." These thoughts gradually overwhelmed her, and she became obsessed with the belief she had been discriminated against because she was a woman and unjustly deprived of what was rightfully hers.

In this situation, her normal behavioural inhibitors were cast aside, and she convinced herself that if the Bank would not recognise her monetarily, she was justified in taking what was her due.

This was a classic scenario for staff fraud – a disgruntled employee with opportunity and motive.

Sue knew the payroll system inside out and the internal auditor's sampling methods. She planned accordingly.

Within the Admin's staff quota, there were several individuals who undertook holiday reliefs and covered absences.

To achieve her ends, Sue selected one of these people, Maxwell Arthur Taylor to duplicate on the fortnightly pay schedule but in a slightly different form using "Tayler M.A." The fact that the genuine individual was a "floater" meant she could place the fraudulent identity anywhere among the Divisions. The similarity was designed to mislead a reader into thinking that the misspelt name was simply a typing error.

At the time, there was no requirement to seek identification when opening bank accounts. To access the proceeds of the fraudulent payroll payments, she set up an account with another bank in the name of Margaret Ann Tayler.

A former State Manager plagued by complaints about privacy had restricted access to the salary printout. For this reason, the Human Resources Officer, Therese Briden, who should have had access was excluded. She, of course, was ideally placed to pick up the duplication but was denied the opportunity to do so.

In any case, there were some 90 odd names on the pay schedule not in alphabetical order as was the formal Admin's staff list but broken up in Divisional format and then in order of seniority.

This cumbersome arrangement implemented in times past, quite apart from anything else, made any comparison using the alphabetical staff list an arduous task.

Albert Wright, the internal auditor, had been doing the job for years and was close to retirement. He had never been ambitious and was comfortable in plodding along doing just what he had to do. But he was too comfortable and lazy!

Wherever he could, he took the easy way out. In this instance, the padding out of a payroll with a phantom employee is a common fraudulent ploy frequently highlighted in audit literature such as textbooks. Any auditor worth his or her salt should be aware of this and recognise the potential risk. Albert wasn't.

The need for a full check was included in the audit syllabus but because "it was too hard" was performed piecemeal and accordingly lacked the necessary rigour.

For her part, when compiling the payroll schedule, Sue always made sure that the duplicated entities were kept well apart.

She knew that Albert restricted his check of salary payments to a sample from a single Division. If he did happen to include the bogus Tayler M.A. in his sample, these details conformed to the bogus Head Office advice in the file she had set up to cover such contingency. Importantly, she also knew from his audit ticks on the salary printout, that he never checked the full Admin's staff list to the complete payroll payments, a check that would have thrown up the duplication.

She of course, would have known the game was up if he had ever sought the complete list. But he didn't!

Sue, shrewdly, also made a point of staying on close friendly terms with Albert. He, as an older widower well past his prime, was flattered that a younger woman would take the time to frequently chat with him.

Albert signed off on the full check after he had separately checked each Division over several weeks, totally oblivious to the fact that his piecemeal approach left the door wide open. It was difficult to understand how he did not grasp the need for a full check notwithstanding its difficulty.

It certainly raised the suspicion when matters finally came to light that he was in cahoots with Sue. When he came across the Tayler entry, as Sue intended, he just accepted it was a typographical error.

Sue's husband had left her for a younger woman. Following her divorce, she had lost self-confidence and had let her appearance slip. This changed when she started accessing the fraudulent funds. She went to the gym and started looking after herself with expensive clothes and pampering.

It is an axiom in banking that management should be continually alert for indications of fraud. Therese Briden headed the Staff Section of which Jimmy Harper and Sue Carney were part. She was one of the few women who had broken through the "glass ceiling" at that stage and whilst not of managerial status, she was the Admin's most senior female. She was very conscientious and alert for anything untoward.

One morning she approached Flite expressing reservations about Sue Carney whose circumstances had seemingly greatly improved over recent times. A little while back, she had been dowdy, taking little pride in her appearance. But this had changed, and she was now a fashion plate. Additionally, her hair, make-up and nails were now always beautifully done.

Alert to the possibilities, Therese mentioned that when passing Sue's desk a few days ago she had deliberately complimented her on her appearance. Quite unflustered, Sue had replied with a giggle that she had met an older wealthy man, "her sugar daddy," who was very generous towards her.

Therese commented that her explanation seemed reasonable enough at the time. However, this morning at tea, she had overheard Sue telling her friends that she had a new car, a British racing green coloured two door Holden Monaro. This was a flash, expensive car and Therese putting it all together, decided she should mention it to Flite. He agreed it was certainly a red flag.

When they enquired, they found out that Sue had not taken holidays or a day off for more than a couple of years. They were also told that she regularly promised to take leave and reduce her leave accumulation but always cancelled at the last moment.

With this additional information, the red flags were flying.

When they looked, there was nothing in her ABC Bank staff account of anything untoward. Certainly, there were no money flows consistent with big spending.

The ABC Bank did not issue its own credit cards but had an arrangement with one of the major banks to issue cards on its behalf. Sue's limit was only $1,000. There was not much leverage there.

Flite grilled the Internal Auditor who strongly denied any fault, claiming he had fulfilled to the letter all his obligations in respect of the payroll. It was obvious though that if there were fraud, it had to be somehow connected to the payroll.

So as not to show his hand, Flite decided he and Therese would conduct their own check of an evening after everybody had gone home.

The first thing Flite noted when he compared the full staff list to the payroll print out, was that whereas the salary printout showed 93 entries, the staff list recorded 92 which was the NSW Admin's formal staff quota. They had hit pay-dirt. Ticking off the names from one list to the other, they soon uncovered the Taylor/Tayler duplication.

The next morning (Tuesday) they did nothing to indicate anything was wrong. Flite informed Simon Sinclair who was not pleased. When the payroll schedule was presented for authorisation, Flite confirmed the presence of the proposed fraudulent payment to Tayler M.A.

When confronted, Sue brazenly tried to bluff her way out, claiming the entry must have been on payroll schedule before she had taken up the job. Unless there had been a necessary adjustment, it would have remained as is. She denied any involvement.

Her defence was blown away when Flite checked with the bank where the account receiving the fraudulent payments was opened.

It confirmed that this occurred when she was well and truly on the job two and a half years ago. Confronted, she broke down and confessed, bitterly criticising management for discriminating against her.

The fact that she was a woman did not figure in the Head Office assessment for the position but reflected the performance reports of Jimmy Hooper's previous department. Simon Sinclair firmly rejected this criticism and told her she was barking up the wrong tree.

She exonerated Albert Wright, the auditor, from any involvement describing him as a "doddery old fool."

All in all, she had got away with best part of a hundred thousand dollars. She was charged, convicted and sentenced to five years gaol.

In gaol, she undertook a university degree in industrial relations and when she was released secured a job as a trade union advocate. She had always been aggressive and soon made a name for herself as a nasty, relentless antagonist of employers. She became a regular union spokesperson and commentator. She never looked back.

Albert Wright having reached the minimum retirement age was asked to go. When questioned why he hadn't conducted the full list check, he fell back on the excuse that it was too onerous to do so. Whilst there was some validity in this, it should not have deterred him. More damming, however, was that he ignored the possibility of ghost employees believing Sue Carney was a "good person" and would never intentionally do anything wrong. The man was totally devastated to learn his trust was so badly misplaced. Nevertheless, apart from this, he was clearly "past it" and obviously should not have been continuing in such a vital role.

Obviously, where money is concerned you must be alert to all risks and cannot afford to trust others to be as honest as you.

THE LAW IS OFT SAID TO BE AN ASS

So, don't be surprised when you are confounded

Lindsay Kelly was a successful rails bookmaker. He lived in a big home in Kensington not far from the Royal Randwick Racecourse. He was known for his generosity towards deserving causes.

Lindsay banked at the ABC Bank's Kensington branch. Each Friday afternoon, he and his assistant Tony Parkes would visit the branch and cash a cheque to cover his "bag" for the morrow's races. Very rarely, he might send Tony back to the branch to cash a further cheque for a couple of thousand odd to top up a particular cash denomination.

But this changed and much more frequently, Tony cashed a further cheque. On each occasion he always explained that they did not have sufficient of the denomination requested. It became a regular occurrence. The branch teller never thought to query why this was happening so frequently after they had cashed their main cheque earlier the same afternoon and had not got the mix right then.

One Friday afternoon, after cashing Lindsay's top-up cheque Tony was greeted by the publican of the Kensington Hotel who was collecting his coin change needs for the weekend's trading. When the teller subsequently asked how he knew Tony, the publican mentioned that he virtually lived at his hotel in its gaming room, playing the pokies and betting on the TAB.

The teller mentioned it to his Manager asking, "Shouldn't we tell Lindsay?" The Manager's response, however, was that was Tony's private business. In any case, Lindsay was a wily bird and if anything, untoward was going on, he would soon pick it.

On Monday, after the usual bookies' settling at the Tattersall's Club Lindsay and Tony would deposit the bag cash at the branch.

In Lindsay's books, Tony (as his bookkeeper) recorded the combined total of the two encashments as the bag cash for the particular race meeting. He noted on the bank statement against the second entry, "Top-up of short denomination."

Lindsay kept control of the cash he and Tony withdrew. At the racecourse, he alone took the money bets and paid out the winners.

At the close of each race meeting, the bag cash was placed in Lindsay's safe at home. His substantial cash holding was thus held securely under his control at all times until it was banked.

The cheques being cashed by Tony were relatively small in respect to the overall volume of money involved. However, the total began to add up.

Lindsay did not closely examine his bank statement. He knew in round figures what the balance should be and if that equated reasonably close to that figure in thousands he made no further enquiry.

Lindsay's Accountant when preparing his annual tax return, delegated the job to a junior clerk in his office. This young man noted the frequent top-ups on the bank statements and mentioned their frequency to the Accountant. He carelessly fobbed matters off on the basis that the explanation of top-ups was not unreasonable (ignoring completely their regularity).

When the Accountant and his clerk visited Lindsay to go through the return with him, the clerk could not restrain himself. Much to the Accountant's displeasure, the young man mentioned the frequency of the top-ups and commented that he could not understand why there were so many. "Well yes", he said "I could understand it happening a couple of times but not nineteen in 8 months.

Lindsay was momentarily confused and asked, “What are you talking about?”

When shown the bank statements, he immediately denied their authenticity adding that he could not remember the last time he had sought a top-up. They were obviously fraudulent. All up, they totalled $32,000.

When Tony was called in and confronted, he tearfully confessed to the theft and his gambling addiction. He was arrested, convicted and sentenced to 3 years gaol. Lindsay was deeply disappointed that Tony, whom he had treated very well, had turned on him in this way.

When he got to thinking about it all, he realised that the Bank had also played a big part in his loss.

In the first instance, the top-up cheques must have borne a forged signature. Additionally, there were a lot of them and as the Accountant’s clerk had pointed out someone at the Bank should have wondered why they were short of a particular denomination so many times and queried this.

When he approached the Bank and examined the signatures on the forged cheques, he had to agree that they all looked genuine. He queried though why the additional activity had not raised their suspicions. In response, the Manager pointed out that the transactions were clear on his Bank statements, and he would have readily noticed them if he had perused them. It was obvious he had not done so, and the loss occurred because of this. But when Lindsay spoke to his solicitor, he confirmed he had reasonable grounds to sue the Bank and so he went to Court.

The Bank strongly denied any negligence. It had provided regular monthly statements that showed the fraudulent entries. Thus, the onus was on Lindsay to peruse them and pick-up anything untoward. However, this might-be-thought common-sense defence was on shaky ground.

Lindsay's highly paid barrister pulled a rabbit out of the hat pointing out that in the 1968 case of Craddock v Selangor Rubber, the Court had ruled that where there was unusual activity on a Bank account outside the norm, it was incumbent upon the Bank to refer to the account's principals.

In Lindsay's case, top-ups had been infrequent for a long time. Yet when they became more frequent and bearing in mind the flimsy repetitive nature of the excuse given for them, the Bank should have been put on notice. It wasn't.

The Bank case was further eroded when initial proceedings were reported in the media. Much to the Bank's horror, the publican of the Kensington Hotel came forward to testify that he had on one occasion mentioned to a bank employee that Tony was a frequent visitor to the hotel's gaming room playing poker machines and betting on the TAB.

When this was confirmed, the Bank conceded. The Court subsequently awarded Lindsay substantial damages. In addition, the Bank was ordered to pay costs. An expensive lesson!

Lindsay, vindicated, took his business elsewhere.

So did the publican.

The Accountant's junior clerk was given a hefty rise for having the courage to speak out and disclose a fraud which might otherwise have gone undetected.

Understandably this decision did not go down well with the banking fraternity as it withheld any onus of responsibility on the plaintiff for his/her lack of personal diligence regarding their account.

But that's the way it is.

TIMOTHY FLATTERY

A Belfast Man

One individual well remembered well after he left the Bank was Timothy Flattery.

Timothy was not Australian but was born and bred in Belfast. Unfortunately, he was disadvantaged from the outset as his family were numbered amongst the Catholic minority who were continually under siege from the rabid Protestant community who were politically and economically dominant.

Northern Ireland is part of the United Kingdom of which Belfast is the capital city. When the predominantly Catholic southern part of Ireland gained independence in 1916, the largely Protestant Northern Ireland provinces remained within the United Kingdom.

Not surprisingly, bearing in mind this background, Belfast society was deeply divided on sectarian lines, a festering state-of-affairs that harkened back for a long time. The deeply embedded animosity on both sides was evident in everyday life and manifested itself in discrimination for jobs and housing and at street level with frequent violence, street brawls even rioting and murders.

The British Army had been called in to help restore some form of order. If anything, they had worsened the situation and frequently worked hand in glove with the Government's Ulster Constabulary against Catholic minority interests.

Timothy's parents ran a small pub in the safe Catholic Falls Road area, safe because nearby streets had been barricaded to prevent incursion by British troops or Ulster constabulary security forces.

Nevertheless, they were constantly on the alert for Protestant troublemakers particularly as the pub was frequented by militant republican sympathisers who actively conspired to bring about the unification of the northern British provinces with the rest of Ireland.

Timothy grew up into a big lad and played rugby in the second row with the Ulster Club. He was good, played aggressively and was identified as an up-and-coming player for the national side.

When he was 18, he was selected to play for the All Ireland Under 19 team against the touring Australian Schoolboys. It turned out to be a real eye-opener for Timothy, very conscious of the bitter religious divide in his own community.

During the game, one of the Australian second row forwards was badly winded and sat for a minute to settle himself. His big second row mate came over and said to him "Listen Johno, you lazy Protestant Yobo get back on your feet. I can't beat these little green men on my own!" Without another word he pulled Johno up, gave him a bear hug and packed down into the ensuing scrum with him.

The Irish boys including Timothy were non-plussed. Here were two individuals, one insulting the other in a religious way but neither they nor any of their teammates seemed to have any worry about it. If it had happened in the Irish team, all hell would have broken out.

As it happened Ireland broke the Australian's unbeaten tour record by a field goal on the bell. At the formal get-together after the game Timothy went over to the two Aussie second rowers skylarking together on a couch. They were obviously good friends.

Timothy said to Johno "if it is not a sore point can you tell me why you did not get upset when he (pointing to his partner) called you a 'lazy Protestant Yobo'?" Johno laughed and hugged his partner. "He's me mate son! We go to Church Schools, mine is Shore, Anglican, his is Joeys Catholic. He is a bloody tike, blesses himself before a game, goes to Mass on Sunday.....but so what! We don't give a rats.....he is me mate and we stick together through thick and thin. We live close by one another and have known one another since we were in kindergarten. Back home, no body or only a very few, are religious bigots and get excited about it."

Timothy was intrigued, but what about the community you live in, your neighbours? He was assured by both the Australians "that there's none of this shit like you have here, back at home."

At home that night in bed, with the sound of gun fire in the distance, Timothy wondered.

After Timothy left school, he did not want to work in the pub and tried for white-collar jobs. He had done well at school, presented well but his catholicity doomed him. He ended up working as a brickie's labourer. If nothing else, it strengthened him physically and toughened him up.

It was inevitable that he would be approached to join one of the Republican para-military groups. When they did one evening when he was serving behind the bar, he agreed to join with his other mates from school and rugby.

Much to his surprise, however, after receiving some basic military training and going out on a couple of relatively harmless forays against the Ulster Constabulary, instead of continuing in the struggle in Belfast he was directed to join the detested British army.

The purpose of this was so that he could learn about weaponry and soldiering generally and come back and pass on to his colleagues, the proper military techniques.

And so, Timothy sailed across the water to Liverpool and joined up. In basic training at Catterick in North Yorkshire he quickly showed he had the makings of a good soldier, strong, tough, and well disciplined. He quickly mastered infantry weaponry. To his surprise, he showed potential as a marksman and was identified for further training in this role.

This training was hard and intensive in harsh conditions, but Timothy persevered. In due course he qualified as "marksman" the highest Army rating by achieving a score of 85% for the whole of the shooting test and got to wear the coveted marksman shoulder patch.

He was then sent to undertake specialist sniper training in an isolated area in the Scottish Highlands covering such areas as advanced marksmanship, field craft and camouflage.

He did well and at the end of his training instead of being appointed to a regular unit he was retained at Sniper School as an Assistant Instructor with corporal rank. After a couple of years in this role, his expertise was recognised, and he was made Instructor and promoted to sergeant.

In April 1982, Argentine troops invaded the Falklands in the South Atlantic to occupy territory they considered theirs. The British Thatcher Government responded quickly and sent a mixed military force of divisional strength to restore their sovereignty drawn from resources readily available.

Timothy and three other instructors were co-opted and joined the expedition attached to the 3rd Para troop Brigade. In the normal course in combat, an individual sniper is assisted by a "spotter" who seeks out and assigns targets. He also confirms whether a shot is successful. No trained "spotters" had been included in the Sniper School group and during the voyage to the South Atlantic, Timothy was teamed up with a young Gurkha named Gejung who had some previous sniper training for this role.

Much of the Falklands terrain is treeless open tundra, with occasional ridges and some low hilly country. There are no native trees but some bush such as native box and facine and stands of tussac, a tough strain of grass that grows to a couple of metres. From a sniper's viewpoint, it was ideal country, with camouflage, to lay hidden and unobserved.

Each day after the British forces broke out of their beachhead at San Carlos, Timothy and Gejung were assigned different areas of operations.

They left British lines before dawn in heavy camouflage and took up a position among the tussac and gorse on higher ground where they could observe and assess Argie troop numbers and disposition. They were specifically ordered to refrain from any offensive action that might compromise and jeopardise their reporting of crucial intelligence.

They successfully provided vital detail of Argie defences during the subsequent battles around Darwin and Goose Green, Mount Kent, and Bluff Cove.

There were exceptions, however, when they were directed to take-out Argie troops.

On one occasion at the battle of Goose Green, the 3rd Para troops were storming an Argie bunker complex in typical South Atlantic conditions of scudding wind and heavy blinding rain. The para troops were attempting to move up purposely in numbers but were pinned down by intensive fire from an Argie machine gun on their left flank hidden at ground level by thick tussac. Timothy and Gejung received a frantic call, "Can you get rid of that bloody machine gun?"

Timothy and Gejung hidden on a slightly raised hillock some 100 yards away could sporadically see through the rain, the heads of the two Argies in their dugout nest. The next time they lifted their heads, Timothy fired. The machine gun immediately stopped, and the surviving Argie infantryman spooked by Timothy's killing shot jumped out of the dugout and ran towards the bunker complex. Timothy shot him as he ran.

With the machine gun nest taken out, the para troops quickly overwhelmed the Argie opposition in their bunkers. With the battle over, Timothy and Gejung walked down to the machine gun nest.

Whilst he was physically tough, Timothy was horrified to see that those he had killed were little more than boys. It impacted heavily on him.

As a sniper team they were lucky and went a long time without being spotted by the Argies. However inevitably, their luck could not last!

In June, in the final stages of the campaign, the British forces were closing in on the capital Stanley. Timothy and Geejung had just taken up position when twenty feet in front of them they were surprised by an Argie trooper crawling through the gorse and lying down to watch the British lines through glasses. He was completely oblivious to their presence. Without a word, Gejung put his finger to his lips and slid off sideways without a sound.

The Argie pulled his camouflage mat over his head and lay still. There was no sound. Ten minutes passed and Timothy started to wonder what had happened to Gejung. A heavy rain squall passed overhead.

A couple of minutes later Gejung returned bringing with him the Argie's beautiful Austrian made Steyr sniper rifle and field glasses.

The Steyr was also fitted out with a powerful German-made scope and noise suppressor. He had smashed the Argie's radio. Gejung said nothing just pointed to his kukri Gurkha knife at his waist. Timothy grimaced but gave him the thumbs up.

The Steyr was a real prize, superior to Timothy's AL used by the British Army and regarded by many professionals because of its superior accuracy and reliability in all conditions as the best sniper rifle in the world. The comparable British rifle had the nickname among the troops of the "civil servant" on the basis that "'it only worked intermittently and could not be fired!"

During the day, Timothy radioed back about efforts being made by the Argies to strengthen their position. Their best result was the spotting of two well concealed bunkers that the Brits were able to knock-out with mortar fire before they advanced.

Late in the morning, a couple of Argie officers scanned their location through field glasses. They had lost contact with their man and surmised, correctly, that the Brits had a presence there. Within minutes, mortar bombs started falling around them as the Argies tried to flush them out. Our boys were shaken but unhurt, the impact of the bombs luckily being lost by intervening sand dunes. The bombs did start a fire among the tussac, but the wind blew the flames away from their position further up the slope behind them and soon died out.

It had been bitterly cold all day with low scudding clouds and rain squalls. In mid-afternoon conditions got worse, the wind picked up and at the same time the heavens opened, and it began to rain heavily. Visibility was reduced to a few yards.

Timothy and Gejung started cautiously down the ridge towards the British lines. They kept low below the tussac. A heavy Southern Atlantic fog started to come down and this helped them. Nonetheless progress was slow. They were only halfway down still wearing their heavy camouflage when they were alerted by low voices just ahead. They went to ground.

A few yards down the track were a cluster of large boulders from which could be heard non-British voices, Argies lying in ambush. They were stuck! They knew where they were there but could not get to them. They were outnumbered and without grenades. They could not get past and just had to wait it out, cold, hungry, and thirsty. Timothy was dying for a cheese and onion sandwich and a strong drink to warm him up. Gejung just cat napped.

They laid there watching and waiting for three hours and as dusk fell the Argies decided to give it away. In the thickening fog, their figures were shadowy, and Timothy decided it was better to let them go rather than engage in a firefight where he and Geejung were vulnerable.

As they approached the British lines, in the now dark they flashed their ID lamp and awaited the challenge for the day's password. However, to their horror, there was no challenge response but a fusillade of automatic weapon fire. Both were hit, Timothy in the hip and Gejung in the stomach. He started to bleed heavily. Timothy raucously shouted they were Brits not bloody Argies and the shooting stopped. An upper-class British voice then called "Who are you?" Timothy replied in gutter Belfast Irish which brought an embarrassed "Sorry lad" from the speaker.

Apparently, the unit in the line in the morning had been relieved and the new Royal Marines unit had inadvertently not been warned a sniper team was "out there". Timothy's radio reports had gone to the earlier unit's intelligence section.

They were quickly taken to the casualty station and then ferried out to the converted hospital ship Uganda anchored in Grantham Bay where they were quickly operated on.

Gejung's wounds were serious and became badly infected. He hovered between life and death for a week but could not be saved. His death hurt Timothy. They were participating in battle and injury and death were part and parcel of everyday life. Whilst they had not been together long, they had bonded, and Timothy grieved for his mate.

The bullet Timothy had received had made a mess of his right hip and upper leg muscles and he was repatriated back to Britain. After several operations and convalescence, he was back on his feet again but was left with a slight limp in his right leg. He was declared medically unfit for combat, given a medal, and honourably discharged from the army. He took the Steyr rifle with him.

Timothy returned to Belfast and served behind the bar of his parent's pub. The IRA boys were not happy when Timothy told them he was finished with the "troubles" and all he wanted now was peace and quiet to forget the horrors he had witnessed. He was also heartily sick of the ongoing culture of hatred and bitterness that prevailed on each side of the divided Belfast community, and which caused so much misery and unhappiness.

Reflecting also on his decision not to engage the departing Argies who had been waiting in ambush, he realised this decision had been influenced by a new heart-felt disgust for all the killing and horrors of war.

There was some retaliatory attempt by the IRA to make him a pariah because of his time with the British Army. However, a priest from the nearby Redemptorist Clothard Monastery, who would later play an important role in negotiations for a lasting cease-fire put a stop to this when he spread the word that Timothy had joined up at the IRA's behest.

Timothy experienced serious post-combat anguish about the senseless slaughter and maiming of men. He drank but it did not help. He turned to God and that did not help either. At his wits end, he recalled his rugby days and the Australian schoolboys. Could it really be any better in Australia?

The pub's barmaid had a sister there who had given her a glowing account of life in the southern suburbs of Sydney, the weather, the beach, easy going people and good housing and jobs. She had not encountered any religious animosity. She reiterated what the Aussie boys had told him "that is that there were no problems with religion like there is back home".

Timothy was convinced, packed his bags and following a raucous, very drunken and maudlin farewell at the pub, said goodbye to his parents and caught the plane to Sydney.

He arrived in early November, and it was like everything he had been told. He stayed with the barmaid's sister and husband in the Sutherland Shire in southern Sydney until he found a job and went off on his own.

He went job hunting. He did not have a trade and did not feel suited for a clerical job. His gammy leg prevented him from undertaking physical work.

Where was he going to find a spot? At the Returned Servicemen's club one evening talking to another Brit vet, it was suggested he contact the British Legion. When he did, his interviewer told him "I think I have just the spot for you. We have placed half a dozen of you boys there over the years and they are all happy."

A couple of days later Timothy received a call telling him an interview had been arranged for employment as a messenger with the ABC Bank. The recruitment person was impressed with Timothy's smart appearance, his warm personality and beautiful Irish brogue. His application for employment was approved and he was appointed to the Bank's NSW Administration.

He was kitted out and given a three-day training course about the Bank, its operations, and his responsibilities.

When he turned up at the office on a high floor of a building in Pitt Street near the Quay, he was surprised to be personally welcomed by the State Manager.

After a brief talk, he was handed over to Tommy Perkins the Head Messenger to be shown the ropes. After an initial briefing, he was taken to meet the Group Leader, Southern Division, Norman MacLeod whose responsibilities included management of messenger staff.

Timothy was not impressed by the way this little podgy man talked down to him and his intrusive personal questioning. He thought to himself, "That boyo bears watching. I will have to be careful."

When he got down to work, Timothy took to the job like a duck to water, smart as paint, always respectful and carried out his duties competently without fuss or bother. Nothing was a trouble to him. He quickly became a favourite among the staff.

For his part, although he still frequently recalled the horror of the Falklands and the bitterness of Belfast, he started to find himself and enjoy life again.

Irish Catholic families coming to Australia tend to cluster. It was not surprising then that several emigrant families had opted to live in the Shire particularly when the Sutherland Catholic Church honoured St Patrick and the parish priest was an older Irishman from Derry.

Terence O'Brien was a physically tough little man who had migrated to Australia after World War 2. He had worked in the mines in the Hunter and knocked around in a tough environment for a few years before entering the seminary. He was unique among his clerical colleagues in so far as he had knowledge of the wider world and was street wise. He had shown himself to be a good working-man's priest. He had great empathy for people in trouble irrespective of their faith.

The barmaid's sister's family went to mass at St Patricks, and it was inevitable that Timothy would follow suit. He made himself known to Terry who warmly welcomed him to the parish. They became good friends.

Timothy welcomed the kinship of the parish and immersed himself in helping, doing odd maintenance and gardening jobs around the church and parish convent school. There was Terry O'Brien and the other Church people, and he was no longer lonely. It was close to Cronulla beach with a great train service to the City.

He rented until he had completed his probationary period and then with the help of the Bank's staff housing scheme purchased a two bedder apartment. Timothy had been taught to ride a motorbike in the army and to get around he also bought himself an old Norton.

Like many Irish men, Timothy had a good voice and at Terry O'Brien's suggestion he joined the parish choir. He was warmly welcomed by the group consisting of an old widower who was the choir master, an older married couple and two middle-aged married women. The organist was a young woman who taught at the parish primary school next door to the church, Kerry Ross.

Kerry was a petite, dark haired girl in her mid-twenties. When Timothy arrived on the scene Kerry was getting over a long-standing relationship that had fallen apart. She was understandably gun-shy of men, but Timothy's good looks and great disposition won her around. Soon they were a couple, to the choir members and Terry O'Brien's delight.

They married within 12 months and Kerry moved in with Timothy. They looked forward to babies and Timothy was in the seventh heaven! The "troubles" were behind him! But one should never say "never" particularly if you are Irish! It might just tempt the Fates.

It did! As we shall see.

CELESTE (RODRIGUESE) DELIANO

Her Karma

Celeste was eight years old when her parents emigrated to Australia from their native Goa after the Indian Army annexed the 450 years old Portuguese enclave in 1961.

Her father, Phillip, a former policeman in Goa readily found employment with the NSW Police. Mori, her mother, obtained work as a receptionist for an Indian specialist medico. They were frugal people, and it was not long before they were nicely settled and living in a comfortable home.

Celeste was a bright child but even then displayed a precocious character flaw. To her parents' utter shame, she was expelled from her convent primary school for stealing money. In high school, she put this behind her and became a high performing student. In her final Higher School Certificate exams, she finished in the top one percent of the state and gained access to the highly sought-after faculties at Sydney University.

Celeste had grown up to be a beautiful woman. Throughout high school, her friends were adamant that she must become a model. She believed them. Her parents, who had been looking forward to her engaging in a high-status professional career, were deeply disappointed when she rejected this possibility to become a fashion model. Swallowing their disappointment, they sent Celeste off to modelling school.

With her exotic appearance, accentuated by her honey-coloured skin and strangely beautiful pale blue eyes, she was recognised from the outset as a "stand-out". It was no surprise when she was picked-up by a national retail chain specialising in high fashion. With her natural hauteur on the catwalk, she proved an instant success and quickly came to the notice of the high-flyer fashion houses. She soon frequently featured on the cover and in fashion shots in women's magazines and was highly sought after for advertising.

Celeste was pushy and ambitious, did what she had to do when she had to and promoted strongly by her agent was quickly among the top ranks of Australian models.

Having arrived there, it was inevitable that she would be drawn into the social world of upper crust Sydney society attending their functions and appearing frequently in the media. She was vivacious whenever interviewed at these affairs and TV producers alert to her potential, offered her regular spots on panel shows, initially as eye-candy but as time went by for her intelligence and wit.

But she could not help herself. Wherever she was, when modelling or at a fashion shoot whenever she fancied something such as belts, bangles, bags or other accessories, she just took them.

She attracted eligible men from the social set and was regarded as a trophy to be won. But she found these men vacuous and vapid. One by one, she sent them packing. She was waiting for the one who apart from being wealthy had to be her intellectual equal. He turned up in an Argentinian polo team visiting Australia for a series of matches against local teams.

Anton deLlano was a wealthy rancher from an old land holding family who had originally arrived from Spain in the late 18th century. He was suave and handsome in a swashbuckling way and the local women fell over him in droves. He flirted but remained aloof.

He noticed Celeste at a dinner chatting to one of the Australian team he had played against earlier. He knew he was a media baron of some kind but very friendly and sociable. He drifted over and was introduced. She chatted for a minute or two then excusing herself left the two men to themselves to talk to an older couple sitting near the bar. She certainly aroused Anton's interest. He did not talk to her again that evening but watched her as she worked the room.

The next time he saw her was at the last game of the series talking to another woman. Anton was not playing following a bad fall during a game in which he had broken his critical right wrist. Picking up a bottle of champagne and glasses from the bar, he walked over to the women and asked if he might join them. With the champagne, he was readily invited to do so.

The husband of Clarice, the other woman, was playing in the current game and rated a 4-goal player. She was somewhat overwhelmed when she queried Anton to learn he had a 9-goal rating.

She explained to Celeste that the rating was a form of handicap, with a player's rating deducted from the team total in the final assessment of scoring. She mentioned that there were only 9 or 10 players with a 10 rating and perhaps a dozen with a 9, which put Anton within the top 20 in the world.

They talked about the game and life in Argentina. Celeste realised that Anton was a "nice man" (and rich). She readily accepted his invitation to dinner the following week. This was the start of a whirlwind courtship over the following six months culminating in their highly publicised media wedding at St. Mary's Cathedral.

They honey-mooned in Spain and then returned to Anton's home on the northern pampas of Argentina to start their married life together.

Anton's widowed mother and two elder brothers welcomed them but were taken aback at the colour of Celeste's skin (exclaiming privately, a "mestizo", a person of mixed blood).

The original deLlano family to settle in Argentina were sons of an eminent grandee of the Spanish peerage. The family was proud of their high status deriving from these forebears and over the years had avoided any taint of "lesser" blood by restricting their marriage partners to Peninsulares (Spanish born persons who later settled in the Americas) or Criollo (persons of Spanish or other European descent born in the

Americas). It did not matter that Celeste had no local indigenous blood; she was still perceived as a "mestizo." This was of no moment to Anton's two older brothers who were entranced and enthusiastically accepted her. His mother, however, was lukewarm and thought Anton had married beneath himself.

The deLlano family were very wealthy deriving mainly from their large beef export business. Apart from large cattle estancia (ranch) holdings, they also owned vineyards known internationally for producing fine malbec wine. Management was split with each of the brothers responsible for specific operations.

The British had been introduced to polo in India in the 19th century and in turn, they had subsequently brought it to Argentina. The country already had a strong equestrian tradition deriving from the exploits of the legendary gauchos on the pampas and the game quickly gained popularity. Today, among those countries where polo is played, the Argentinians are well recognised as the world's best.

Because of the associated expense (particularly the need for a string of highly bred and trained horses) it is a sport for wealthy men. Nevertheless, it has a huge following in the country.

Anton managed three large estancias on the fertile northern pampas where beef cattle, mainly Angus, flourished. His home was located some 50 kilometres west of Curuzo Hauti in the Chaco province. The hacienda was a beautiful white stucco home surrounded by red flowering trellised bougainvillea. It was furnished with rich Spanish style dark furniture, its solemnity broken by a delightful array of tasteful carpets, curtains and cushions.

Celeste was delighted with everything particularly the score of Indian servants who were receptive to her every wish. There was a beautiful, tiled pool and large stables. Language was something of a problem, but she soon grasped enough to make herself understood.

Anton had taught her to ride in Sydney, regularly taking her to ride in Centennial Park. Now home in Curuzo, after breakfast they would regularly ride around the estancia. Anton would then go to his office or visit other ranches or cattle sales. In his absence, Celeste would swim in the pool or lay by it reading. Occasionally, they would entertain or visit a nearby estancia owned by friends of Anton for an elaborate BBQ lunch or dinner.

Their social life quickened up during the polo season which ran from October to December. Quite apart from the polo, there were always BBQs or dinners afterwards at which Anton delighted in showing her off. For her part, Celeste enjoyed the adulation and attention paid to her by the menfolk. Her attractiveness also did not go unnoticed by their wives and partners and their jealousy certainly did nothing to help her cause for friendship.

The women at these functions were friendly enough but when Celeste tried to make friends, she was politely rebuffed.

Anton regularly left home for a week at a time on family business supervising his other properties and arranging the selling off of cattle for the export market. Celeste never accompanied him. Occasionally, they would visit Buenos Aires for a few days to shop and get a break from the sameness of life on the estancia.

Anton continued to treat her well and obviously still loved her. But Celeste was devoid of women friends with whom to confide and consort. She missed the closeness of women companionship of her own kind and the regular social life she previously enjoyed. She started to grow restless and disenchanted with her life on the pampas.

She was also deeply disappointed that she had not been able to conceive. Anton did not seem too concerned but the inability to have children deeply grieved her.

Her depression grew. One evening at dinner she broached with Anton the possibility of returning to Sydney to see her parents and catch up with old friends. It was more than four years since she had left Australia and apart from other issues, she was homesick. Anton readily agreed. Business commitments presently prevented him from accompanying her, but he promised he would join her in a few weeks.

So, off she went. When she arrived at Sydney airport and was met by her parents, she burst into tears, overjoyed to be "home". She dutifully spent a couple of weeks with them.

Then, as she caught up with and partied with old friends, she quickly fell back into the social whirl she had left behind and sorely missed. She realised she preferred this to her somewhat lonely life on the pampas.

She also visited a specialist gynaecologist who confirmed that there was no reason why she could not conceive. The medico queried her concerning Anton. Celeste was aware that he had fathered a child in his late teens with one of the family housemaids. The child had subsequently been adopted out to an English family through an adoption agency.

On learning this, the medico suggested that Anton might be taking steps to avoid her pregnancy. She shook her head. He couldn't be! Surely not? He shrugged, threw up his hands and said, "I have told you what I think. You need to give it some thought."

Reflecting on this subsequently, the realisation suddenly struck her. Anton did not want to have children because she was mestizo! Any child she bore would have mixed blood. Realising that this was the case, beyond any doubt, she was heartbroken.

Anton telephoned her to say he could not join her as planned and she told him she didn't care. They were finished. He was devastated and came to Sydney as quickly as he could, dropping everything else. When confronted, he admitted he had had a vasectomy to avoid children with her. Even so, he loved her.

Incensed by his total lack of empathy and selfishness, she angrily told him she had lost all respect for him. He had wilfully deprived her of the fulfillment of children that every woman craves and in doing so, her love had simply evaporated. She was adamant, she was not going back. He returned alone, heartbroken.

They divorced. The Argentinian Court was not as generous towards women as in Australia. Whilst Anton was worth in his own right some $US 40 million excluding his share of the huge family cattle business, Celeste was awarded only $2 million.

When she returned to Australia, unbeknown to Anton, she brought with her not only the jewellery he had lavished on her but also his family heirloom Spanish jewellery, necklaces, rings and earrings, worth thousands. She had wanted to show it off and would have returned with it, if she had gone back. But she didn't.

When Anton had come to Sydney to plead for her return, he had no reason to suspect that this jewellery was held otherwise than in its special safe in his office. The key was in his desk drawer. He never married again and there was never a woman in his life to wear this jewellery. He thus had no cause to look in the safe and did not discover the theft for many years.

For Celeste, this jewellery made up somewhat for what she saw as the meagre settlement figure she had been awarded. She had no intention of giving it back.

She had an unexpected windfall with the penthouse apartment in the ritzy suburb of Double Bay she had purchased some 12 months prior to her marriage. While close to the Harbour and even though she was on the top floor of her building, her view had been largely obscured by two older blocks of units directly in front.

In her absence, however, developers had moved in, demolished the apartment blocks and built a row of exclusive two-level town houses. She now had an unparalleled view straight up the Harbour and an apartment that had doubled in value.

Since she had left Sydney she was now four years older, and modelling was no longer an option. However, she was remembered by TV executives and now possessed some exotic veneer deriving from her sojourn in Argentina. She picked up regular TV work. Apart from the money, it maintained her high social profile.

Whilst she was still beautiful, she was no longer the eagerly sought prize of five years ago. She was not attracted to the older (even though wealthy) men who attempted to court her.

Celeste was used to the advantages of money, of getting anything she wanted and living the high life.

She was welcomed back to Sydney's top society. However, to maintain her place, it was important that she had the trappings that went with it. She paid off her mortgage and shopped around locally, looking at investment options. In the end, dissatisfied with local prospects, she placed her residual funds amounting to $1.3 million in a Swiss Bank investment fund she knew of through her association with Anton.

Prior to her marriage she had bought her clothes from a little-known fashion house in Mumbai that specialised in copying the latest designs from Paris and Milan at a fraction of the original cost. Word of its existence was restricted locally to a coterie of women in the top fashion echelons and social strata. Now back in Sydney, she got rid of her dated Argentinian clothes and replaced them with the Mumbai firm's high fashion.

Her next step was to acquire an up-market limousine. She knew nothing about cars, but she wanted something very big and showy. At the next A-List function, she talked to a well-known media presenter who was known to collect vintage cars. When he learned she would not be driving it, he suggested a 1976 Eldorado Cadillac, presently a few years old, but very eye-catching.

He knew of one for sale in Melbourne and on his recommendation, she bought it sight unseen for $50,000. (Brand new in the USA it cost

$US11,000). It was jet black, in mint condition and just what she wanted. With this beautiful car in her garage, she then looked for a part-time chauffeur. She found him driving a taxi, a handsome young Sikh.

At the next big red-carpet TV affair, she made a grand entrance, turning heads and eyes green when she alighted from her magnificent limousine in a gorgeous figure-accentuating gown assisted by her red turbaned handsome chauffeur. It was classic "style" and the paparazzi loved it. "She was back in town."

Being a realist in respect to money, Celeste recognised that her TV income and Swiss Bank investment would not sustain her in the long term. She needed to get money behind her. A lot!

Her shrewd mind started to weigh up the options and inherent risks. Earlier, she had opened an account with the local ABC Bank branch and talked about local investment options with a financial advisor. This woman had cautioned her about dubious investments. In particular, she warned against getting involved in Ponzi-type schemes where high returns were promised but the arrangements were spurious, and the promoters abscond with your funds.

Rather than serving as a warning, it prompted Celeste to think about such a scheme as a possible get-rich ploy. As far as she was concerned, it did not matter that it was illegal. Her priority was to get her hands on a lot of money quick. After a little reflection, but without any pangs of conscience, Celeste opted to start her own scheme and prey on peoples' greed.

As a first step, she started to entertain lavishly selecting her dinner guests carefully, people in the public eye earning big money, top actors, sportsmen as well as wealthy friends and acquaintances. At these dinners she wore the latest overseas fashions and her Spanish jewellery. Her guests were dazzled and invariably the question arose as to how she could afford to live this way.

She conceded she had received a good divorce settlement and went on to explain that she was receiving excellent returns, very much more than what could be obtained locally from a Swiss Bank investment fund.

When her guests sought more information, her spiel was persuasive extolling the high rate of return and the security of dealing with a strong 150-year-old bank with an international reputation. It was inevitable then that she would be asked whether it was possible for others to share in this investment bonanza.

The fish were nibbling at the bait!

When asked the question, she was cautiously hesitant explaining that access was very selective, and she did not want to do anything to prejudice her situation. Then after a minute's pause of supposedly deep thought, she hooked the fish saying, "I can't see much harm though in enabling a few of my friends to also benefit."

She explained that because of the nature of arrangements they could not gain entry in their own right and their funds would have to be in her name, in her account. However, to protect their interests and provide comfort she would arrange for a co-signatory on the account to ensure she could not run-off with the money.

Thinking aloud, (although she already had it in mind) she suggested that perhaps someone like Abe Goldman, a well-known eastern suburbs rabbi and spokesman for the Jewish community would be ideal. Her potential investors thoroughly agreed. Whilst Abe subsequently signed an authority form, Celeste never lodged it with the Bank.

The money started to roll in.

She provided her investors with a copy of each half-yearly bank statement showing total funds invested and a (bogus) certificate showing a fictitious current value of their individual investment and the percentage increase since last reported. Prima facie, the return was excellent well in excess of local expectations.

On a few occasions, investors sought return of their funds and Celeste quickly arranged this, ensuring that the amount lodged to the investors' bank accounts included the high fictitious return.

When her scam had been operating for three years, Celeste decided to review her financial position. She had accumulated some $8 million of other peoples' money. These funds together with her own $1.3 million, had benefitted from the normal (but much lesser than promised) return on funds. All up, funds with the Swiss Fund totalled close to $10 million.

Her unit was probably worth a little over a million. She decided she had enough. She was also losing her nerve and was apprehensive about getting caught if she continued much longer. She quietly put her penthouse on the market and accepted the first offer of a million.

She visited her parents and told them she was going overseas for a working holiday. When she left the family home and unbeknown to her mother, she took her passport and driver's licence.

On the day after settlement of her apartment sale, she transferred the funds to her Swiss Bank account. She quickly followed this up with instructions to forward all funds to a large Indian bank in Mumbai with the request "to hold for arrival of payee from overseas and pay on identification."

The next day she asked her Sikh chauffeur to drive her to the airport. Once there, she signed over to him the registration papers for the big Cadillac. She left him gob-smacked and in tears.

She paid cash for a flight to Brisbane using her mother's driver's licence as identification. That evening she cut her hair short and dyed it grey. She removed all her makeup.

The next day she flew to Port Moresby. The Indian lady wearing a sari, dark glasses and walking with a stick did not attract any undue attention. Three days later she arrived in New Delhi via Hong Kong and Dubai. Having used her mother's passport, she was now Mori Rodriquese.

She visited the Mumbai bank and identifying herself with the passport, arranged for the remitted funds to be credited to an account in that name. There was clearly a strong resemblance between her face and the photo in the passport and this aspect was never queried.

She bought an attractive apartment in the up-market Navi Beach area. With her residual funds and prudent investment, she knew she was set for life in Mumbai. She also knew that living under her mother's name, there was little chance of discovery.

In Sydney, her disappearance and discovery of her scam were sensational news. The Federal Police sought her (under her deLlano name), but she had concealed her tracks well. When she could not be found and seemingly had not fled overseas, it was believed Celeste had gone to ground somewhere in Australia.

When the Swiss Bank was contacted, it's only response was that it held no accounts in the name of Celeste deLlano. It did not disclose the destination of transferred funds in that name.

She joined the Mumbai Polo Club. As an attractive, single, wealthy woman who knew the game of polo it was not long before she attracted several older male admirers. Within months, she married an Oxford educated long time bachelor who was a director of his family's container shipping line.

She now wore a sari and adopted her husband's name fully conscious of the fact that this made tracing her even more difficult.

Twelve years passed during which time she produced twin sons and settled down to the life of a wealthy matron. She was happy and content.

In her and her husband's beautiful home high on Malabar Hill in an up-market gated community, she was well insulated from the vapours and undesirable aspects of the densely populated city. Nevertheless, she was not immune from diseases such as cholera that regularly plagued the general population.

Cholera is an infectious disease caused by a bacterium that typically lives in estuaries and waters along coastal areas like Mumbai constantly befouled by garbage and sewerage. People contract it after drinking contaminated water or eating foods such as raw or undercooked shellfish.

Not everybody who comes in contact with the bacterium becomes ill. However, those that do, experience severe diarrhea and vomiting which lead to serious dehydration and septic shock. If not treated properly, death can occur within a few hours.

When an outbreak occurred on one occasion, Celeste became very ill and seriously dehydrated. She was at death's door. Her husband, greatly concerned, quickly arranged for the best medical care and she survived. However, she had been badly knocked about and her subsequent recovery was slow. She had lost a lot of weight and her body had shrunk noticeably. She had aged considerably in the process.

This Saturday afternoon she was alone and depressed. Her husband was at a shipping conference in Delhi and sons away in boarding school. She decided to visit the polo club, knowing there were always people there she could have a chit-chat with and help buck herself up.

When she arrived, she met up with a couple of girlfriends sitting on the club's balcony watching polo on the ground below. She ordered a gin and tonic and started to feel better. When the game finished, her friends went downstairs to meet their husbands.

As she watched them leave, she saw this man get up from his table near the door and stride towards her. With a sudden shock, she recognised Anton. Belatedly, she remembered that an Argentinian team was visiting the club. She frantically asked herself, "God, what am I going to do?"

When Anton came near, he said tersely, "So, Celeste, this is where you have been hiding? I have been looking for you for a long time so I can get my jewellery back." Then with a sarcastic laugh, he added, "I have no doubt too, my dear, that those poor people you stole money from, will also be very interested to learn where you are."

Celeste quickly pulled herself together and decided to bluff it out. Looking Anton straight in the eye, without any indication of recognition, she replied, "I don't know you sir, whoever you are. My name is not Celeste but Mori. I did have a daughter named Celeste from my first marriage. She got into trouble in Australia, and I think she is still there somewhere. So please do not pester me. I am not her."

Anton noted that this woman, now close up, was older than he expected, had grey scraggy hair, wore no make-up and was wearing a sari. She looked and acted like any Indian woman. Certainly, there was a resemblance but of course there would be. Celeste's mother should now be in sixties. This woman was very thin and frail. It was hard to gauge but she could be anything. Sixties was not out of the question.

Anton was certainly put off by this unexpected outcome. He had first noticed her from a distance a few days earlier and thought he recognised Celeste. However, now that he saw her close up, she was different, older and claimed to be otherwise. Was he mistaken?

Embarrassed, he muttered an apology and left the club. Back at his hotel, he tried to figure out whether it was Celeste? He had only met her parents a few times before they married and now had no memory of what they looked like. Yes, there was a resemblance to Celeste, but this woman was unlike what he had anticipated her to look like.

The Celeste he knew, was a vain, fashion-conscious woman and was always dressed and groomed immaculately. He could never imagine her appearing in public or in the salubrious premises of the Polo Club looking like this person. Importantly too, this woman today had showed no surprise or recognition when he confronted her.

In the end, he concluded he was mistaken. It was not Celeste.

For Celeste, even though she had put up a bold front, was badly shaken. She had no doubt that whilst she had temporarily pulled the wool over Anton's eyes, he would sooner or later realise it was her and reveal where she was. In any case, she would not give him back his jewellery. She had a couple of gins and tonic and went to bed. She could not sleep twisting and turning with worry. Her world was in tatters. She was about to lose everything.

The next morning when the house maid brought her coffee, she was not there. Her car was gone. The house maid surmised she had gone to visit friends. But she did not come home that day. When she had not shown the next day, the house maid telephoned Celeste's husband.

Aadav was 12-year-old. He lived with his widowed mother and elder sister in a one room, dirt floor shanty of makeshift material on the western edge of the Mumbai slum enclave of Dhavari near the police station. They had no services such as sewerage, electricity or safe drinking water. The community bath house and public toilets were 100 yards away.

Dharavi is one huge slum, perhaps Asia's largest. It has a population of about a million all living closely packed together. Sanitation is poor and clean water is scarce. In these conditions, it is inevitable that serious outbreaks of disease are commonplace.

Whilst there is extreme poverty, there are many household businesses producing items such as leather goods, textiles and pottery, even some foundries employing local residents.

Nadia, Aadav's mother, was typical of many. She worked long hours, seven days a week for low wages in a sweat shop sewing clothes for an internationally known brand of sportswear. The family eked out a miserable existence on her meagre wage.

To help, Aadav had made a fish trap and set it daily in a small clump of mangrove close to the foot of the Mithi River Bridge a couple of miles away.

The Mithi River is today badly polluted from raw sewerage, garbage and industrial waste and marine life has long gone. The river has been deteriorating for many years but at this time, its condition was somewhat better. Fish were still fairly plentiful, and the poor marine environment had not yet deterred their consumption.

Each morning before the sun rose, Aadav would ride his dead father's rickety old bike to check his trap. When he came to the bridge, he climbed down the rock embankment buttressing its side and waded into the mangroves. The water was up to his chin. He ducked under, picked up his trap and waded back to the water's edge. This morning, he was lucky, there were two good sized fish. He gutted and cleaned them and reset the trap.

He was wading back to the riverbank when something black caught the corner of his eye to his right. He froze thinking it was a shark that had come into the river to feed! But no, it didn't move towards him.

It was a woman's body. (Celeste! She had jumped off the adjacent 20-foot high Mithi River Bridge and had come down hard on the shallow, rocky riverbed.)

There was nobody around. He dragged the body to the water's edge. Strapped to her back was a small, heavy knapsack. When Aadav opened it, inside was a veritable treasure trove of jewellery. Too scared to look more closely and very excited, he emptied the contents of the knapsack into his dillybag. Then after strapping the knapsack back on the body, he filled it with dirt from the riverbank and pushed it back into the water. The body sank a little but remained close to the surface.

Aadav, frightened, hurried home. He was scared what his mother would say. When entered the house, he called, "Aaii (Mum), come and see what I have. I hope you are not going to be angry with me, but I think we are rich!" His mother disappointed him, crankily demanding, "Did you catch any fish?"

Crestfallen, Aadav handed over the fish. His mother commented that they were good fish and placed them in the family's one iron cooking pot. After sprinkling them liberally with salt and curry spices she added a little water and placed the lid on the pot. Then seeing Aadav's disappointed face, she put her arm around him and said, "Come on now my wonderful son, show me why we are going to be rich."

Then, with his mother and sister sitting with him on his bed mat he emptied the contents of the dillybag. They sat there dumbfounded. There were four heavy gold necklaces studded with precious stones, strings of pearls, gold chains and bracelets, rings and earrings. There was no doubt that what lay before them represented an immense amount of money. Aadav's mother threw her arms around him and said through tears, "Yes, my son, we are going to be rich!"

Aadav told them how he had found the jewellery and truly, they agreed, it was a windfall from the gods. They were not going to tell the police in the nearby station about the body or the jewellery.

And so, taking their time and careful not to attract attention, they sold off their trove piece by piece to the many fences in the enclave.

Even though they were invariably robbed blind, they gradually accumulated a lot of money with which they bought small gold bars and buried in cooking pots.

Their quality of life improved and they never went hungry again. They opened a market stall where tourists visited. It prospered selling copies of a well-known sports clothing brand made by Nadia. They were now financially secure.

They knew of no life other than in the enclave and they were not inclined to move away. They did, however, move to a better two room house without the inevitable blue tarpaulin on the roof to keep out the monsoonal rain. The house was connected to electricity, and they bought a television to watch Bollywood movies. The community bath-house and public toilets were only 50 yards away. Life was good.

The irony of it all, of course, was that Celeste had no need to kill herself. Anton had returned home convinced that the woman he spoke to was her mother. She had fooled him. He never learned he was mistaken and that his brief confrontation had led to her death.

Celeste's body was found later that same morning and identified from her name tag and phone number on the knapsack. Her husband was inconsolable, and he and the sons went into mourning. He loved her dearly and never got over her tragic death. Often, he would sit looking out over the city and wondered why this had been her Karma.

This concept is deeply embedded in Hindu culture. In the West it is widely misunderstood. However, in simple terms, it embodies the belief that the consequences of our actions impact directly on our lives, now and in the future. Specifically, good actions bring good future outcomes: bad deeds bring bad consequences. In other words, you reap what you sow.

In Celeste's case, she was a thief from an early age. She had hurt many people including her parents and friends. Her unnecessary suicide triggered by the mistaken belief that her past would be revealed was indeed a fitting Karma she deserved.

SIMON SINCLAIR - STATE MANAGER

It's Great to be The King!

This particular morning, Simon Sinclair called an early meeting of his senior executives to inform them that they were being visited by a prince from one of the smaller Arab states who had been spending a few days with the Bank looking at its organisational structure and governance. He had already spent time at Head Office but was visiting the State Admin today to gain some insight first-hand as to how it fitted into the overall scheme of things. He was flying home tomorrow.

His family was one of the ruling elite, exceedingly wealthy with substantial oil and banking interests. The prince, in fact, was a director on the board of the family's middle eastern bank with an international reputation.

He had been royally entertained elsewhere and was somewhat tired of all the fuss. He had declined any formal board function and indicated that he would be very happy for something low key such as a visit to a suitable CBD restaurant as the guest of a younger senior executive. He said that as today was his last day in Australia all he really wanted was to relax a little over an enjoyable meal.

Simon Sinclair mentioned that he and Les Ferguson would spend time with him to brief him on the Admin's state role. When that concluded, Flite had the job of looking after him and his bodyguard and to take them to lunch. The provisos were that the restaurant must be up-market, that there must be no scantily dressed women nearby and definitely no pork.

Flite took off to a fancy "suits" restaurant in Pitt Street called the Pink Cloud managed by a tall willowy American blonde called Hank.

She was a very competent woman and within a few minutes she had set up a special table, roped it off and appointed a waiter to look after them. She explained the embargo on pork and the waiter indicated that this would not be problem.

In the meantime, the prince had turned up and was discussing the NSW Admin's operational role and relationships with Simon and Les.

These talks ended at a quarter to one and the prince indicated he would like to go to lunch.

Hank welcomed them warmly and led them to the roped off area with a separate table for the bodyguard. They studied the menu. The speciality of the house was a mixed grill....a piece of succulent steak, a lamb cutlet, sausage and an array of prime vegetables.

The prince confided that he really enjoyed Australian lamb and beef. They had meat at home, of course, but not like here. So, they decided on two mixed grills. The bodyguard opted for a vegetarian meal.

Flite queried the waiter as to whether the sausages were pork and after referral to the chef, he returned to say they were beef. As he was going, Bill reiterated that there was to be no pork involved. The waiter assured him somewhat disparagingly that he was quite aware of what he had to do.

Flite and the prince started to converse over orange juice. It turned out that he had played cricket when he was at school in England and was a real fan. He was playing regularly in a local competition back home.

Then their meals turned up, looking wonderful, the only trouble was that across the top of each plate was a slab of grilled bacon.

Quelle horreur!

The prince jumped to his feet and called out as if he had been hit. Flite jumped to his feet yelling at the waiter "You dope, don't you see what you have done!" The bodyguard grabs Youssef pushes him against the wall and stands in front of him.

There is pandemonium. Hank comes running down from the front desk and sizes things up immediately. She grabs the plates, shoves them into the hands of the now terrified waiter and tells him to get them back to the kitchen.

Hank is a real beauty and good talker and within a couple of minutes she has quietened things down and they return to their seats. She is all over Youssef who loves it. Yes, he will still have the mixed grill but laughingly "no bacon"!

In time the meals return, and they get stuck in.

They start to talk cricket again and it is obvious that the prince is right up on what is currently happening in the game. Continuing from before, he tells Flite that whilst he loves batting he aspires to being a good leg break bowler. He went on to say that one thing about the ethics of the game had always puzzled him and asked whether Flite might clarify.

When Flite said he would try, Youssef asked, "What is the right thing to do when you have snicked the ball and are caught behind by the wicket keeper, but the umpire gives you 'not out'. What do you do? Do you walk or not?" He explains from his English schooling experience, he understands that cricket is a gentleman's game, and it is most proper to do the right thing. In these circumstances, wasn't it correct "to walk?"

Flite laughed and agreed that in times past, you would. However, in today's extremely competitive world, you must take advantage of whatever Dame Fortune dishes out. You have got to take the good with the bad. Sometimes you are given out when you are not and there are other times when the reverse happens. Things even out! "In my view" he said, "you play hard and never walk!"

When they return to the Bank, Flite was understandably concerned the bacon disaster would emerge.

But nothing is said.

Whilst enjoying coffee with the senior executive group, the prince decides to go to the bathroom. Whilst standing at the heads, he reassures Flite that everything is fine and that he loved the mixed grill. He tells Flite he really enjoyed himself particularly the bacon bit as it will give him something to talk about when he gets back home. He loved their talk about cricket and Flite's comment that "You play hard and never walk!"

In the meantime, Flite has asked his people to buy a couple of the latest cricket books. Youssef is delighted and thanks Flite profusely. He and the bodyguard are all smiles when they leave. Flite heaved a great sigh of relief.

A fortnight later, the senior executive was having morning tea with the Bank's Deputy Managing Director when Timothy, the reception messenger popped his head around the door to announce that there was someone out the front to see Flite from an Arab Embassy. As it happened, Flite was in the middle of a presentation and Simon Sinclair went out to see the visitor.

When the Deputy Managing Director departed Simon called Flite into his office saying this package had come from Youssef. It was a small beautifully packaged parcel but bore no addressee. The enclosed card simply said, "Thank you for looking after me so well – Youssef". Also enclosed was a watch which Simon proceeded to put on but noted on the reverse the inscribed words 'You play hard and never walk.' "I wonder what that means?" he commented....as his phone rang and he dismissed Flite.

It was a Tag Heuer, one of the world's best sport watches. It was obviously intended for Flite but while the embassy courier had asked to see him there was no addressee on the package. Flite hesitated and wondered if he should say something. However, without his name on the package, he knew he would be battling to convince Simon of his claim irrespective of the inscription.

Yes, it is great to be the King!!!

EDWARD JOSEPH (TEDDY) CHOMLEY

A Young Man Growing Up

Edward Joseph (Teddy) Chomley was a wild kid. He marched to his own drum and his professional parents had great difficulty keeping him in check.

The family lived in the Sydney harbourside suburb of Rose Bay. He was spoilt rotten and had this bad streak in him. He was constantly in trouble.

When he was 10 and for some twelve months thereafter, he frequently broke into neighbours' homes stealing money, confectionery and anything he fancied. He was also not loath to sample any hard liquor left out on bar shelves.

He was only caught once and that for the last time, when he disturbed the family's Doberman which bailed him up on the kitchen bench until the owners came home from shopping an hour later. The neighbours, of course, knew who he was and rang his parents to come and get him. Knowing they were highly respectable people, they did not report the matter to the police. His deeply ashamed father came and took him home after apologising to the house holders.

When confronting his mother and father later, he confessed to his spate of break-ins over the past 12 months. Profoundly shocked by his aberrant activity they sought professional help to rid him of this behaviour. No doubt this helped but what really deterred him from further burglary ventures was his confrontation with the Doberman. The dog was big and ferocious and had terrified him out of his wits.

This, however, did not stop him from further erratic behaviour. In sixth class, whenever he was in trouble, he would shin up a downpipe and sit on the school's roof until it was time to go home.

When it was time to start high school, his concerned parents hoped that living under closer discipline and supervision than they could provide, might pull him into line. So, with that fond hope, he was bundled off as a full-time boarder at a nearby elite college. It worked! There were some seventy new young fellows all as potentially wild starting off, accommodated in house dormitories on campus with students from preceding years. He had to conform. If he or his peers caused trouble the whole first-year class House group were penalised. In this way, the cohort were coerced into behaving. Teddy quickly recognised the reality and fell into line.

He threw himself wholeheartedly into the School's sporting activities, developed strong friendships and thoroughly enjoyed boarding school life. In his final year, he was a member of the School's premiership winning rugby first XV and rowed bow in their G.P.S. Head of the River champion eight. Whilst he did not apply the same weight to his academic studies, he nevertheless finished in the top third of his class and gained access to Law at Sydney University.

His parents were justifiably proud of him. But it did not last. Whilst he passed his first year Law exams, he dropped out from Uni immediately afterwards. He did not like it!

His mother was a solicitor and one of her male clients seeking divorce, was a senior branch manager in the ABC Bank who spoke highly of making a career there. His parents suggested it to Teddy. Whilst not particularly enamoured with the idea, Teddy went along with things on the assumption that it would be an easier life compared to slogging through more years of Uni.

No thought was given to his earlier aberrant behaviour or that him becoming a bank employee might be likened to leaving a kid unsupervised in a lolly shop. If it were thought about at all, it was assumed he had got it out of his system. And they were right.

He certainly did not put a foot wrong as he progressed through the various stages of becoming a fully-fledged banker. He performed well. When he was 30 and had been in the Bank for ten years, he put his first foot on the promotional ladder and was appointed Assistant Manager at Ashley Grove branch some 10 minutes drive from where he was presently living.

Ashley Grove is the most elite suburb on Sydney's touted north shore. Residents there are affluent, often powerful people, judges, partners in legal firms, senior public servants, Macquarie Street medicos, senior corporate executives and retirees of the same ilk.

A retired Board Chairman of the Bank also lived in the suburb and that was primarily the reason why the branch remained open. Whilst it did hold substantial funds it had no lending business base. His wife used to like walking the 200 yards from their home to do her banking business at "her husband's bank".

The branch's only worthwhile account was Henri's Superior Grocery Store renowned Sydney-wide for its magnificent range of high-quality food and beverages.

Teddy was happy enough; he was not hard pressed and had ample money with his bank pay regularly topped up by his parents. He was living with Trish, a striking young woman who was a journalist in the newsroom (and sometime weather girl) at a nearby television station. He was head over heels in love with her. After he had left school, he had played first grade rugby for several years with the prestigious Gordon Rugby Union Club. Now that he had retired from playing, he maintained a strong association with the club and enjoyed the strong social camaraderie that existed among former players. He seemed settled. There was no more bizarre behaviour. He was a reformed character.

His parents were gratified with his new persona and congratulated themselves on their choice of schools. They frequently commented to each other that it shows you what a good college education could do and agreed it WAS worth all that money.

CHARLES COOPER DFC. DSO.

An Honourable Man

Charles was Teddy's Manager at his new branch.

Charles had been born in Australia of English parents. When world war broke out in September 1939, Charles just turned 19 was in London with his Mum and Dad visiting his maternal grandparents.

Within a few days of commencement of war, he had enlisted in the RAF and with his even then superior airs was selected for pilot training with the Empire Air Training Scheme in faraway Rhodesia.

He had no difficulty completing the basics on Tiger Moth aircraft and progressed to advanced training on the single engine North American Harvard (a "cousin" of the controversial 1940s Australian made Wirraway, designed as a trainer but disastrously thrown into combat as an "emergency" front line fighter early in the Pacific war).

The Harvard was a successful training aircraft, but it had its own idiosyncrasies particularly when landing in cross winds. In these conditions, it was best handled not in the conventional way but by a controlled approach whereby the aircraft was stalled just above the tarmac so that the tail hit the deck first to make a perfect three-point landing. The technique was taught to all pilot trainees.

Charles had had previous difficulty with handling the plane but had persevered and improved both in skill and confidence. However, when he had almost completed his training and gained his wings, he pranged. He was landing in very windy conditions and didn't do it right bringing the Harvard down too hard on the tarmac. The under carriage collapsed under the impact and the aircraft made a skidding belly landing. The aircraft was quickly repaired but he spent two months convalescing with broken legs and experiencing a total loss of confidence in his flying ability. If things could not get worse, they did.

During his time in hospital, he learned both his parents had been killed in the London Blitz. He mourned alone.

Every trainee entering the Air Training Scheme was keen to be a pilot. Whilst there were barely enough of those coming through, with the heavy losses of crews in bombing operations over Europe there was also a pressing need for other trained personnel such as bomb aimers, radio operators, navigators.

When Charles returned from his injuries, the "head shrink" people determined that there was no time for him to regain confidence and he was scrubbed from pilot training. He was unceremoniously bundled off that program to become a bomb aimer.

He was a natural and quickly acquired skill in this art. So much so, that his capability came to the notice of the experimental group on the base developing a much-needed bombsight for Bomber Command. To his surprise (but on the recommendation of the Base Commander) he was invited to join the group and be their aimer in tests using an ageing Blenheim bomber lent by the South African air force. The eventual final design resulted in vastly improved accuracy and was quickly adopted by Bomber Command for all its operational aircraft. Charles received commendation for his role and for a suggestion concerning magnification that was incorporated in the final design.

He graduated his year as top trainee overall and in view of his achievement acquired the junior commission of Pilot Officer.

In February 1941, Teddy returned to England and joined a newly established heavy bomber squadron being formed with elements of RAAF personnel drawn from an existing squadron originally raised at Williamtown in Australia at the start of the war.

Before joining the squadron, Charles spent a few days with his maternal grandparents mourning the loss of his parents and visiting their graves. He also received an earlier letter from his father's executor in Sydney reassuring him that the substantial estate was in good hands.

Charles' squadron was at that stage flying twin-engine Vickers Wellington heavy bombers on night missions over Germany and Occupied Europe. He joined an Australian crew that had already made some ten missions. Charles was replacing their bomb aimer who had been killed on that mission by shrapnel from a near-miss of anti-aircraft gun fire.

He and fellow crew members undertook some ten missions together, bombing Dusseldorf, the Ruhr, Dortmund, and Essen and even two to Berlin without any real problems. However, their luck did not last.

On their next raid, over Berlin, everything had gone well. Despite intense ack ack fire, Charles guided his Skipper directly over the target area lit up by incendiaries dropped by an earlier flight and hit the button to release their bombs. Immediately the plane rose up with the loss of weight and the Skipper echoing the thoughts of all on board muttered through the intercom "Thank God for that. Now let's get home" turned and headed west.

The ack ack explosive puffs stopped and as they did so, swarms of lurking night fighters attacked the bomber flights. Out of nowhere, a black twin engine ME 110 appeared on their starboard and blasted the Wimpey with a long burst of cannon fire. The result was disastrous. The skipper who was piloting the aircraft was killed outright at the controls as were the nose and waist gunners.

Charles was seriously wounded in the right thigh.

The fuselage was like a sieve with holes everywhere. Worse still the starboard engine was crippled and now and then a long ribbon of smoke would stream from it. Their remaining port engine did not falter and seemed undamaged. The instrument panel, however, was a mess with nothing working. They were losing height.

Charles, moving with great difficulty and pain, dragged the pilot away from his seat with the help of the radio operator. Thanking his lucky stars, he had had some pilot training, he took over the controls.

He was, of course, totally unfamiliar with the controls of the Wellington aircraft, his difficulty further compounded by the fact that he was also flying this heavy bomber on one engine. He was flying by the seat of his pants and a great deal of intuition.

He regained a bit of height and luckily found some cloud cover to avoid the enemy fighters.

The radio operator's head had been badly gashed by flying debris and he had got a dressing on it. Blood kept running beneath the dressing and he had to continually wipe it away. He, Charles, and the tail gunner were the only ones alive.

It was still dark but reasonably clear with a pale moon. They were by themselves. There was no sign of the other Wellingtons that flew with them earlier. Their remaining operative engine spluttered intermittently but each time happily returned to full power.

They had no idea of their fuel situation. They had no working instruments.

Normally, Charles would have been able to navigate but wounded and needing all his time to fly the plane this was impossible.

Fortunately, they were able to pick up landmarks in north western Germany recognised from previous raids, ticking off on their map what they thought were the towns in question.

They were in fact further south than they thought due to the torque of their single engine. When they came to a river that they both agreed was probably the Rhine, they managed to turn hard and follow it north. After a short while to their utter relief, they could see Rotterdam over to their left and the North Sea ahead of them.

Without warning, a ME 109 German fighter lurking specifically to catch night stragglers pounced. His first strafing run astern shattered their tail section and killed the rear gunner.

Their remaining port side engine spluttered a couple of times and lost power but again recovered.

They were a sitting duck with no chance to hit back. Charles thought to himself “this is it” and waited for the coup de grace. But it did not come. They had little time to wonder because in a matter of moments they had a wonderful looking British Spitfire fighter alongside them, the pilot giving them the thumbs up. When the “spit” turned up the ME 109 immediately broke off and scurried away to his base in Northern France. The Spit had been lurking in the area to catch any German fighters waiting to pick off stragglers. Talk about double think but so fortunate!

They crossed the white cliffs and with the aircraft shuddering and shaking badly and on the verge of stalling, landed safely at their base in Lincolnshire.

Charles was incapable of moving. He was bleeding heavily and physically exhausted. Two medics had to extricate him and put him on a stretcher. He could not walk.

The two medics carrying Charles and the radio operator had just exited the bullet-ridden fuselage and the bodies of their dead comrades placed in an ambulance when the starboard engine exploded in flame engulfing the whole aircraft.

Charles was traumatised by it all and apart from his wounds he also suffered combat stress. He spent three months in hospital convalescing and undergoing psychiatric care.

While still in hospital he was visited by his Commanding Officer and told that because of his heroic effort in bringing the crippled aircraft home he had been promoted to Flying Officer and awarded the Distinguished Flying Cross. The citation specifically mentioned that despite being seriously wounded, his lack of formal pilot qualification and unfamiliarity with the controls of the Wellington, he had shown great courage and determination to successfully bring the severely damaged plane and crew back home.

He was invested with his medal when King George VI visited the hospital to thank the injured RAF aircrew who had been taking the war to the German homeland.

The evening after he had been released from hospital and returned to base, he and the radio operator celebrated at the squadron's favourite water hole, The Marquis of Granby pub. The motherly woman publican welcomed him back warmly, sewed his decoration patch on to his jacket and opened a scarce bottle of French bubbly, on the house, to toast Charles and his award.

He had recovered successfully on all counts and when declared fit for duty, his flying potential was recognised, and he underwent formal pilot training on the new Avro Lancaster heavy bombers coming on stream.

He completed this training successfully and completed his remaining tour missions unscathed, piloting and skippering the same Lancaster aircraft "D for Donna," the name of his flight engineer's wife.

They had a few close calls. Once when they came under friendly fire from the rear gunner of a Lancaster immediately ahead of them. The gunner was bringing his guns around to meet an attacking Focke Wulf 190 coming in astern to starboard but panicked and inadvertently started firing before he had got his Browning guns sufficiently in position. His fire hit their starboard wing but fortunately did not damage either of their two engines there.

Damage or worse from friendly fire was not uncommon on large raids with hundreds of planes flying close.

So too were collisions and pilots had to keep their wits about them.

Their last tour mission together was a raid on Berlin. They were just coming in to bomb over the red flare markers left by the pathfinder Mosquito aircraft when one of the new jet ME262s hit them with cannon fire and flew over them at tremendous speed a few feet above them. The speed had obviously deceived the pilot because most of his cannon fire passed over them. It did, however, strike their far port engine which immediately lost power. It intermittently started to emit a stream of thin white smoke. The Lanc bucketed in the ME 262's slipstream and with only three engines operational Charles momentarily lost control. A violent last second yank of the controls enabled them to avoid collision with the Lancaster flying abreast on their port wing.

They were then close to the target, seemingly not in any immediate danger so they pressed on. After finessing their position, the bomb aimer was just releasing their bombs when another or same ME262 almost collided with them at last moment veering quickly. Charles also reacted instantly and pulled the Lanc away. The bomb aimer let off a string of profanities as his bombs exploded away from the target area.

Again, they watched, as the ME 262 flashed down just ahead of them and attacked another Lancaster which burst into flame, turned over burning and fell out of the sky.

Charles with the help of his Flight Engineer cut off the fuel to the disabled engine. Successfully feathered, the stream of smoke stopped.

The rest of the trip proved uneventful, and they returned safely to base on three engines with no real difficulty and without casualties. All told, Charles concluded, that was a good last day at the office.

They reported the incident with the ME262 and that their bombs had inadvertently fallen outside the target area.

Charles' elation at completing his tour was shattered the next day when to his horror, Berlin Radio accused British Bomber Command of another indiscriminate bombing atrocity. It appeared that their off-target bombs had fallen on an orphanage killing children and nuns sheltering in the building's cellars.

Charles and his crew were subsequently exonerated of any fault in the RAF enquiry. Nevertheless, the disaster cast a heavy pall on their normally jubilant spirits for having survived their operational tour.

This revolutionary German jet fighter ME262 was to prove a deadly menace in the closing months of the war. Fortunately for the Allies, German authorities had concentrated on production of bombers and delayed its introduction. If it had been deployed in numbers earlier, the heavy bombing campaign that the Allies were able to conduct might well have been significantly reduced, an outcome that would have undoubtedly prolonged hostilities.

Charles finished his tour in July 1944 just after D Day and the Allied invasion of France. Granted a fortnight's leave, he took off on one of the base's motorcycles and rode down to a little fishing village in Cornwall he had heard about.

Gunwallowe was a small, scattered village with a population of less than 200. He booked into the old Helzephron Hotel reputed to have been a haunt of smugglers and wreckers in years gone by.

For the first couple of nights, Charles quickly fell into a heavy sleep in a wonderful soft bed. He was lethargic and had no energy. After a couple of good night rests, he felt sufficiently relaxed and decided to go to the bar each evening and have a couple of drinks before going to bed.

The barmaid was the publican's daughter, Penelope. She was about the same age as Charles, slim, pert, and friendly. He had taken out a couple of girls along the way since he joined the RAF but had not got serious with any, in view of the tenuous nature of his existence.

But now his tour was over, he felt he could be more serious about relationships.

He responded to Penny's flirting and for the rest of his leave in Gunwallowe, they were together every day. He found himself increasingly attracted to her.

He enjoyed her company and particularly her love of classical music which he shared. Of an evening, they would sit in the parlour listening on the pub's crank handled gramophone to her collection of classical records enjoying the music and each other's company.

On his last evening before returning to base, he had had a couple of scotches at the bar, kissed her goodnight with feeling and gone to bed. About half an hour later somebody soft, warm, and smelling delightfully got into bed beside him and snuggled up close. It was a naked Penny. They made love and afterwards talked softly to one another listening to the wind and rain. Charles was over himself happy. Though they had only been together a few days, he knew he had found someone he could be happy with. To his delight, Penny felt the same.

When he returned to his base, his Commanding Officer told him he was required at RAF Head Quarters. On arrival, he was congratulated on completing his tour and was then asked (very jovially) would he like to do it again. When Charles exclaimed "Lancasters?" with a sinking heart, his two interviewing officers laughed and said "No! What about Mosquitos?"

They went on to explain that with the invasion of France well under way since D Day there was a pressing need to learn what the Germans were doing to counter Allied armies ahead of their advances. For this reason, the RAF had a pressing need for photographic reconnaissance, and they were pushing more resources into this operation.

The aircraft used in this role was the versatile twin engine jack of all trades De Haviland Mosquito. The Mosquito was very different beast in that its fuselage was constructed mainly of wood with two powerful Merlin engines. When it first became operational, it was one of the fastest operational aircraft in the world. It remained so right up to the end of the war. Originally planned as an unarmed fast bomber the Mosquito's use evolved during the war into many roles including photoreconnaissance. In this form, it was unarmed relying on its speed and manoeuvrability to evade German fighter planes.

The RAF was careful in the pilots they chose for this aircraft restricting selection to well experienced proficient flyers who had demonstrated their capability. Charles had received several commendations during his tour and was perceived as an ideal candidate. When he agreed, he was whisked off quickly to undertake a conversion training program for the Mosquito and to learn the art of photoreconnaissance. His earlier bomb aimer training and operational experience put him in good stead. He breezed through this training quickly mastering the idiosyncrasies of the aircraft such as the yaw to the left on take-off due to engine torque. He relished the lightness of the controls and the speed. He quickly grew to love flying it.

Within weeks he had joined his new photographic reconnaissance squadron which had moved to France after the Allied break-out from Normandy. He was regularly flying over eastern France filming German defence preparations ahead of the advancing Allied armies.

When his Mosquito was fitted with radar he undertook night missions. He also performed photo flights over targets deep in Germany to ascertain damage of recent bombing raids.

His stay over photographic targets were invariably of short duration, at low level and completed before German defences had time to respond. Whenever he did encounter German propeller driven fighter planes he just put his foot down and out-ran them. Fortunately, he was never confronted by the formidable (faster) ME 262 jet fighter which undoubtedly would have made mincemeat of him.

With the quicker shorter missions, he undertook them more frequently than when flying Lancasters. His mission tally rose quickly, and he completed his second tour in March 1945.

He was now a Squadron Leader and considered himself fortunate to have gained that rank. However, RAF Command recognised his contribution in successfully bringing back detailed photos of German military installations particularly those of German V2 rocket launch sites, from which Hitler had been terrorising London. His and other revealing photos obtained by fellow squadron members had enabled Bomber Command to destroy these sites and free the city from this scourge. He was awarded the Distinguished Service Order for meritorious service in active operations against the enemy. Penny, her Mum and Dad together with his grandparents were thrilled to bits and accompanied Charles to his investiture by King George at Buckingham Palace.

They all celebrated together at a lavish luncheon at Claridges featuring new season caviar and lobster and French champagne. Charles paid the bill.

As the Allied armies advanced, his squadron moved to Belgium and then to the Netherlands. It spent the last months of the war photographing shipping activity along the Dutch and German coasts.

Having completed his second tour in March, Charles remained grounded until the end of hostilities in May and took no part in these operations. Whenever he got short leave Charles would hotfoot it across the Channel to Cornwall and Penny. They had fallen deeply in love and spent as much time together as they could.

Whenever she was off work during the day, he would take her on his motor bike to hike and picnic around the bays enjoying the beautiful peaceful coastal surrounds.

With the European war over, preparatory planning had started for the squadron to move East to take on Japan. Charles with two tours behind him was not involved. He was a free agent and he spent most of the time at Gunwallowe.

Following the dropping of the atom bombs in August 1945, Japan surrendered. The squadron disbanded in October. After he was demobbed,

Charles remained in England courting Penny and trying to remove the aftermath of constant stress and trauma of his war experience. There were also the self-recriminations, the accidental bombing of the orphanage in particular frequently coming back to haunt him. He was also facing the dilemma of whether to return to Australia and if he did, would Penny come with him.

With his parents now both dead, he had inherited their impressive home on the Hunters Hill peninsula together with his stockbroker father's substantial share portfolio in blue chip stocks. He was wealthy in his own right and reflecting on things, he could see that he could make a go of things in England. But he did miss Sydney, the harbour, sailing his skiff, the warmth and sun and the freer and easier lifestyle.

At Christmas, Charles asked Penny if she were prepared to leave her home in Gunwallowe and come to Australia with him if they married. She readily agreed.

Charles went through the traditional ritual of asking her father for his consent and then having received that, on Christmas Day at the pub's celebratory lunch he popped the question to loud applause from all present. Penny was blushing beautiful as he slipped the massive diamond ring on her finger.

They married in May and after a honeymoon in Scotland they set off for their new life together in Australia.

In his absence, his father's solicitor had leased the family home as an Anglican Church-run convalescent hostel for wounded veterans returning from the New Guinea fighting against the Japanese. When Penny and Charles first visited, it was decidedly run down. Whilst it was in a great position facing up a river, after the small Cornish houses Penny was used to, it was huge. They sold it for an impressive figure to the Catholic Order of Nuns who taught nearby and planned to use it as a retirement home for their aged sisters.

Charles and Penny purchased an older cottage in the leafy suburb of Ashley Grove built from local stone and with a beautiful English garden with lots of roses. In spring, the flowering blue wisteria along the property's fences were magnificent and complemented the many blue flowering Jacarandas in the streets. Penny was entranced and became an avid gardener. She and Charles were very happy.

Charles decided he needed a job. His father's stock broking partner offered to take him on. He was also offered a couple of company directorships through his father's connections, but he turned down them all. With his inheritance, he was now very comfortably placed financially. With all the trauma he had experienced during the past 5 years, not knowing for hours at a time whether the next minute was going to be his last, he yearned for a less stressful life but, of course, with reasonable status.

All the Banks at that time were offering places for returned servicemen. Charles' father's stock broking partner was a director on the ABC Bank's board and at his suggestion he joined it.

With his distinguished war record and senior service rank he was readily recognised as a cut above the norm. He was also being sponsored by a Board Director. Accordingly, his initial placement was not to the rough and tumble of branch life but to the Bank's secretariat as an Assistant Board Clerk.

In this role, he became privy to the inner workings of the Bank at senior level through access to Board reports and submissions and attending its meetings and those of its Sub-Committees. The Bank's Secretary, his immediate superior, noted as time went by that he was smart, good on his feet and self-assured as a speaker (nothing hassled him). He was also impressed by his skill in networking at the top level. The Secretary came to rely heavily on him. Over time, the Secretary pushed him into representational roles such as the Bank's member on working parties initiated by the Australian Bankers Association.

When the Bank's formal spokesperson retired, Charles was seen as the obvious replacement. There he was, a decorated War Hero with a superior confident air, someone who knew the bank's inner workings and culture firsthand and who could not be rattled.

The financial journalists he dealt with were a shrewd, canny, often cruel lot. In their inimitable brutal dog-eat-dog approach, they tried their best to find a chink in his armour. They tried everything in their repertoire to provoke him or force him into an error. His correctness and professionalism, however, beat them and that superior smirk at their antics, irritated them greatly. In the end, he beat them and they, in turn, came to respect him.

His professional performance in this role was well recognised by the Bank's Board and top management. He had found his niche and continued as the Bank's front man for many years regularly appearing on television, radio and in the press.

Charles and Penny remained very devoted to one another. Two years after they married, much to their joy, Penny had a little boy. Charles was over the moon and doted on the bub. They had a good life together enjoying their son, their garden, and their joint love of music. They were regular concertgoers to Sydney's Opera House.

Charles bought a half-cabin sailboat and as often as they could, they sailed on the harbour of a Sunday, anchoring in some quiet cove for lunch and a glass of wine. They were pioneer members of the Hunters Hill Sailing Club where Charles had boy-hood friends and were active in seeing it progress and develop.

Penny's parents came to visit from Gunwallowe regularly and eventually when they retired, they came to live in Australia permanently in nearby Chatswood.

Yes, life was complete and remained so for many years. Jeremy, their son, was a good kid, did well at school and eventually graduated in Medicine from Sydney University. After practising as a surgeon at Sydney's St Vincent's Hospital for three years he had left Australia and had gone to

Scotland to undertake post graduate training in Edinburgh at the Royal College of Surgeons.

Not long after he left, Penny developed breast cancer. Fortunately, they detected it very early and after surgery followed by radiation treatment she went into remission. At this stage, Charles had been with the Bank for some 30 years and had received regular promotion. But Penny was still not travelling well. Somehow, she contracted meningitis and Charles nearly lost her.

When she got over this, she had difficulty going on their frequent long walks and it was found she had contracted rheumatoid arthritis and was very fragile. Charles was worried. He needed to keep an eye on her. He thought long and hard as to how he could do this. He couldn't whilst continuing in town. He was still a few years off retirement age, and it was too costly to resign and forego his valuable indexed pension superannuation rights. He had to get a Bank job close to home.

Flite was his contact within the NSW Admin and he had a working relationship with him. He invited him to lunch at the Limerick Hotel in Macquarie Place close to both their offices and which maintained a good table.

Charles explained his situation to Flite and enquired as to what was the likelihood of a conveniently located branch management job becoming vacant soon. Flite was somewhat surprised at the request in view of Charles' lofty status within the hierarchy. Whilst he readily understood the underlying rationale, he had to point out to Charles that possible branches at his grade were quite senior and some distance away. It was unlikely that they would be suitable for his purpose.

To get a suitable branch close to home, he would need to drop several grades and that might not be palatable. Flite was surprised when Charles confirmed that that would not be a concern. They concluded lunch with Flite promising to investigate possible suitable branches becoming vacant over the next few months.

Charles approached the Bank's Secretary and told him he wished to relinquish his spokesperson role and move to a more junior branch management job so he could be close to Penny. The Secretary expressed considerable disappointment but readily understood.

Flite was as good as his word. At a branch managers' training day, he caught up with the Manager, Ashley Grove (the Coopers lived less than 10 minutes' walk away). Flite was aware this man had said he intended to work through until 65, the ultimate retirement age. Flite discreetly enquired whether this was still his intention. It was not. Probing further, Flite gleaned that he was getting tired and that he proposed to hang up his boots in the next couple of months.

A Godsend! Just what the doctor ordered!

Charles was delighted and spoke to the Secretary. He in turn spoke to the Managing Director who in turn spoke to the Human Resources Inspector. A done deal! As is often the case in banking circles, it's not what you know, but who you know to get on.

When the incumbent manager retired, Charles was formally appointed. The Human Resources Inspector split the difference in grades for which Charles was thankful but had not sought. He subsequently thanked in person everyone who had been of assistance in securing management of this branch on his doorstep.

The branch staff were somewhat apprehensive at his coming. However, they need not have been. Yes, he was pompous, always calling staff by their surname and very correct in his ways but he was fair and treated them well. They came to like and respect him.

From Charles' viewpoint, he was walking distance from home and every day at noon walked home to have lunch with Penny.

His managerial duties were far from onerous. He rarely had loan interviews or difficulties with recalcitrant borrowers. He was meticulous in ensuring his Assistant Manager maintained a sound day to day operation, particularly in respect to security, achieving daily balance and that the required periodical audits and checks were satisfactorily performed.

His main involvement was assisting his older wealthy customers with their banking needs. Sometimes they came to him seeking investment advice.

For many years, Bank managers were highly regarded individuals within the community. One reason for this was the public perception that they knew about financial matters and that their advice was invariably sought before embarking on any new venture. This faith in their financial acumen, however, was ill founded as they had no specific expertise backed up by training or qualification to render such advice.

It was a practice that had evolved over many years and jealously clung to by managers who passed judgment based purely on their own unqualified, subjective assessment. Over time, it was probably their cultural conservatism that saved them and delayed the day of reckoning. Nevertheless, sooner or later, it was inevitable that substantial loss because of relying on wrong advice resulted in successful legal action and awarding of damages.

When this happened, Banks quickly pulled the plug on the practice and adopted a Duty of Care constraint against the giving of financial advice.

In this climate, Charles had to be careful in what he said. If he directly recommended something and it went bad causing loss, he and the Bank could be found liable by the courts. So, when he was approached, he neither endorsed nor advised against the investment irrespective of his own view. He stressed to the clients that as a layman, he was not qualified to express an opinion concerning their proposal. If they needed help in deciding what to do there were individuals and firms holding themselves out to provide such assistance and they should approach them.

Clients invariably recognised the common sense of his response and the counsel he offered. Occasionally, he received thanks from clients for his part in them avoiding a costly mistake.

After 3 years as branch manager, he was relaxed and content.

He was happy when Teddy, a former Great Public-School boy and top rugby player was appointed his Assistant Manager knowing he would be somebody of the same social status and assumably, as honourable as himself.

He, of course, was aware the Chomleys (a shortened form of Cholmeley) were an aristocratic English family with some prominence in English history. He hoped that some of their quality would have rubbed off on this young man.

Teddy, of course, presented himself well, was duly deferential and respectful. He recognised Charles's snobbishness for what it was and played along with it. They got on well together, Charles bending somewhat to call him Edward. He, of course, was always "Mr. Cooper". Teddy performed well and had the branch ticking over nicely to Charles' satisfaction.

The branch had an inspection and audit from the NSW Admin and had received a clean bill of health.

One Tuesday morning soon afterwards, immediately after a long weekend, Teddy did not turn up for work. Charles phoned his home without success.

The door to the branch strong room had two combinations with keyed locks. One set was held by Charles and one by Teddy. Without Teddy, the branch strong room door could not be opened and the teller's cash and necessary records for the day's business activities could not be accessed. Charles knew that Teddy would be aware of this and in accordance with normal practice if he were ill, he should have planned for his key and combination to be delivered to the branch.

Duplicate keys and copy of Teddy's combination number were held in a sealed packet at another Bank branch nearby. These were hurriedly obtained so they could open on time.

But Charles was concerned at Teddy's non-appearance without any contact. It was very strange.

Branch treasury cash is always held in the cash safe in the strong room. Again, custodianship is jointly held by two people, normally the Manager and his Assistant Manager and their two keys are required to gain access. The Bank regularly stressed to staff that keys relating to cash custodianship must be always held securely, preferably on their person. However, the size of key bundles often made this impractical.

A horrible thought crossed Charles' mind. He sighted the treasury cash register and saw there had been a withdrawal the previous Friday signed for by the teller and a purported initial of his in confirmation. But it was not! He went to the cash safe and with the two keys opened the treasury compartment. His worst fears were confirmed. All the larger $50 and $100 denominations were gone.

That bloody young scoundrel Teddy! Still cool calm and collected as he always was in critical situations, he telephoned Flite to tell him.

THE MARQUIS OF GRANBY PUB

Source: Firkins Peter
"460 Squadronraaf.com *Binbrook's Rich History*"
Extract: *"The Marquis of Granby Pub"*

In 1942, 460 squadron was relocated to a new base at Binbrook village in Lincolnshire.

There was much for the young airmen from overseas to see and visit in the area. However, the most popular spot for them by far was The Marquis of Granby pub in the village.

Here they could relax and enjoy themselves for a short while putting out of their mind the trauma and inevitable terror of their highly dangerous bombing missions over Germany and Occupied Europe.

The warm and comforting environment of the Granby was due in no small way to the efforts of the publican, Rene Trevor.

Rene had been brought up living in the Crown Inn in nearby Tealby which her father had run for some 40 odd years. It thus was natural enough for her and her husband to get into the hotel game also. So, in November 1939, just after their daughter, Anne, was born they took over the Granby.

Not long afterwards, her husband joined the army and Rene ran the Marquis of Granby on her own for the rest of the war.

She was a caring woman with a big heart and whilst she was the licensee, she found herself thrust into the additional role of "mother" to hundreds of young Australian airmen.

She sang, played the piano, and took time to console those who grieved or were having difficulty coping with the ongoing trauma of operations.

She sewed on buttons and new decorations, mended jackets and cooked meals for the young men who flew the bombers from Binbrook.

They in turn never forgot her.

The first airmen to arrive at the Marquis of Granby were the crews of the obsolete Fairey Battles.

Rene can remember them saying, "A real English Pub with a piano — can you play it?"

She did and this was the start of a wonderful relationship between the Granby, its landlady and the boys of Bomber Command.

These young men thrust into the horrors of war whilst still little more than boys would walk or cycle down to the Marquis at every evening opportunity for a pint or two of Holes Ale (later Hewitts, Guinness or whatever Rene could get her hands on).

She was always ready to cook her famous meal — sausages, two eggs and toast, for 1s.6d.

After the party was over there would be the riotous departure. Everyone grabbing his bike and setting off mostly in the right direction, with plenty of chiack like "Gawd, give me course navigator, don't know where we are!" or "Oh, don't worry it's all right. I think that's Kings Bloody Cross just up the road a bit" or "Bloody hell, I am up the creek without a paddle, my rear gunner is pissed as a parrot!"

This banter lasted till they got to the hill when it was, "Stuff this, I'm walking home." Then the long straggling line would sing "Show me the way to go home" followed by a plaintive, heartfelt "Good night Irene."

In the morning, the reality would hit as they learned the "target for tonight" and who was going.

Rene often recalled the day the Australians first turned up. We had just been telling my daughter Ann, aged 3, about the war and those nasty Germans.

This day she came running into the back bar screaming "Mummy, Mummy do something those nasty Germans have come!"

Fortunately, it was not soldiering of the Third Reich, but some bloody Australians and she had just heard their accent for the first time.

The odds these young men faced were fearful and the 460 Squadron lost more aircrew than any other in Bomber Command. However, many did complete their 30-trip tour of operations and on each of these occasions there was a celebration at the Granby.

A tradition at these shows was, for those celebrating, for them to be held up close to the ceiling while they recorded their names. Perhaps these and the ribald doggerel are still there.

One piece of such doggerel that is still extant is on the South Eastern wall at face height. It reads thus: -

"If Herr Hitler wants more babies
From his frauliens fair,
Just remember the old motto boys,
Australia will be there."

After the war, Rene lived in a flat on the Cleethorpes sea front. Over her fireplace hung 460 Squadron's Kangaroo and Boomerang crest bearing the motto 'Strike and Return'. "Oh, they were marvellous days" she used to recall. "They were wonderful boys, and I knew just about every one of them."

The village too has not forgotten. In front of its St. Mary's church to this day, there is a well tendered memorial to the 460 Squadron.

THEY WERE VERY BRAVE YOUNG MEN INDEED.

A SMART YOUNG MAN

But not smart enuf

In those days, when another Bank customer wished to deposit money to his/her account but there was no branch conveniently close, he could arrange this through an ABC Bank branch.

The ABC Bank employed an ingenious form for this purpose consisting of three parts with incorporated carbon for details to appear on all three copies.

Each had its purpose.

The third copy was used by the ABC Bank branch who had received the funds to credit a suspense account in its books.

Parts 1 and 2 of the form were mailed to the other bank. They used the original copy as the posting medium to credit their customer's account, with the second copy being directed back to the initiating ABC branch for value. On receipt of this copy, the amount involved would be debited against funds held in the suspense account and transaction would be completed.

It was a simple practice that had worked well for years without any embedded authentication process. Up until this time, in the early 1980s, there had never been any defalcation or dispute. On reflection, however, in the absence of any verification to confirm authenticity by the other bank, the process was wide open.

One smart young staff man recognised the security gap. However, because the transfer form was a behind the counter item and not freely available to the public, he did not appreciate that with any clandestine use, it would be recognised as an inside job.

It all started when ABC Bank branches started to receive "transfer to other bank" form drawings from other banks in the eastern suburbs of Sydney where there was no corresponding credit in the alleged initiating ABC Bank branch books.

All were for five thousand dollars.

The rogue staff member had got around and opened savings accounts at other banks. He/she then mailed a bogus transfer form to the other bank purporting to provide funds for credit of those accounts. Then, before the reimbursement drawing from the other bank reached the ABC Bank, he/she would go there and withdraw the funds. Because the drawing was on ABC Bank paper, it was obliged to honour them and bear the loss, that quickly grew to $25,000.

The matter was placed into the hands of the Bondi Junction police, the investigating officer being a very crusty old detective who had seen everything.

Flite circulated Managers of eastern suburbs branches with copies of the other bank new account and withdrawal forms seeking to identify writing as one of their staff. He did not get a reply.

The investigating officer from Flite's General Section visited the other bank branches seeking a description of the person involved.

Other bank staff were co-operative. All accounts were opened with a $50 initial deposit. Then, about a week later, they received an early call seeking confirmation that the $5,000 had arrived. The funds were withdrawn.

They described the culprit as a young man in his early twenties, well dressed, not too tall and fair headed. A very general description but not detailed sufficiently.

Things were at an impasse. The situation changed when other bank branches in the Sydney central business district were targeted. The ABC's total loss started to climb again.

It struck Flite that the change in target area must mean that whoever the staff member responsible was, he had been recently transferred into the city area. He obtained a list of staff who had been recently transferred from the eastern suburbs into town.

There were a dozen names on the list. After they removed females and persons with Greek, Italian or Lebanese names and assumably had dark hair, they were left with three names.

Two were at city branches, the other was in the Treasury and Accounting Head Office Department.

Flite visited the branch offices in question. One fellow was very tall, with thick black curly hair; the other fellow was bald. It was not them. It now all rested on the staff member at Head Office.

The Group Leader Treasury/Accounting had his chief clerk take Flite's man through the office and close to the staff member who had been recently transferred in from Coogee branch. EUREKA! WITH HIS FAIR HEAD OF HAIR, IT HAD TO BE HIM.

Flite's team member obtained copies of his recent handwriting from his present position and Coogee branch for comparison with the writing on other bank new account and withdrawal forms. He went to see Paul Larkin, the NSW Police handwriting expert.

The next day, Paul confirmed there was no doubt that the handwriting was identical and that he was prepared to go to Court and swear on it.

Flite telephoned the crusty old detective at Bondi Junction. He was not particularly interested until Flite mentioned Paul Larkin was prepared to go to court. His immediate reaction was "OK! Let's go pluck him!"

When the detectives arrived at Head Office, the staff member was called into the Group Leader's office. When confronted, he readily admitted he was the culprit, his only response being to ask, "How did you get to know it was me?"

He was 23, a bright young man already identified as a possible junior executive.

He had traded in his old car and with his ill-gotten gains he had acquired a newish second-hand Honda. But the driving motivation for his criminal rampage was that he had become infatuated with a woman some years older than himself. He was trying to impress her, showering her with expensive gifts, taken her to the fanciest restaurants and bought first class air tickets to Honolulu and booked a suite at the best hotel in town.

He had got away with $40,000 and when he was apprehended had spent $27,000. The Bank retrieved the unspent $13,000 and his parents, who were well off, reimbursed the bank for the money spent.

The case went to Court. His parents engaged top counsel and he escaped with a 5-year good behaviour bond!

No doubt, he got on with his life and went well. He was smart!

The Bank learned the hard way its procedure was flawed and withdrew its transfer form from branches. It no longer offered that transfer facility.

NORMAN MACLEOD

A Bad Man

Norman MacLeod, Group Leader Southern Division was a small podgy man, bald with rimless glasses through which he squinted when talking to anyone.

In seniority, he was number three in the state after the Deputy State Manager but was the odd man out in the executive management group. Norman was a committed Christian, Church Elder and Sunday school teacher. He did not drink nor smoke. He never attended staff functions.

He was full of himself believing he was intellectually superior. He bullied anybody less senior than himself and had the deserved reputation of being a hard man to work for. He had a long background in lending but was excessively pedantic. He was often described as the "wicket-keeper" on the basis that nothing got past him.

ABC Bank's branch managers could approve personal and car loans but had limited authority for anything larger. Consequently, most other loan applications had to be submitted to the state office. It was important then from a customer viewpoint that there was no undue delay in getting decisions back to the branch.

For Simon Sinclair, the Southern Division was a concern. It was constantly struggling to cope with its inflow of applications with decisions invariably taking a day or two longer than in other Divisions. When he sought an explanation, Norman MacLeod laid the blame fairly and squarely on the inferior quality of his staff and their over-processing of applications. This was a surprising call bearing in mind that the Admin's staff were all specially selected. The other Lending Divisions were not having difficulty and Norman's explanation did not ring true.

Erik Neilsen was the Corporate Lending Team Leader within Northern Division when Simon Sinclair decided to promote him to Senior Loans Manager in Norman's Division.

Erik was a strong personality, firm in his opinions and not hesitant to express them when this was appropriate. His performance reports were first class, and he was perceived as a young man going places.

Stan Thompson, whom he was replacing, could no longer tolerate the bullying and constant petty criticism by Norman. He was on the verge of a nervous breakdown and urgently sought a transfer out of the NSW Admin. By shrewdly placing Erik Nielsen, a proven "tough nut" in the crucial Senior Loans Manager spot, Simon Sinclair hoped to learn the true position and get things fixed.

Erik was a likely lad in his early thirties, tall with broad shoulders and a thatch of unruly blond hair. He was not only a no-nonsense character but was also tough physically. He was a long time, active member of the North Bondi Surf Club, presently the Club's Boat Captain and Sweep of their champion senior surf boat crew.

During the winter months, he played with a couple of mates from the Surf Club in the Souths Juniors Rugby League competition with the long-established Beachies Club.

He was a man's man. Whilst over the years he had had several short relationships with women, he had never committed for the long term. Erik was acutely aware that Stan Thompson whom he was replacing had had a hard time with Norman. Being the man he was, he was determined that he would not let that happen to himself.

On the morning of his arrival in Southern Division, he went to see Norman. Entering his office, Erik greeted him by his first name and extended his hand. Norman ignored the hand and snapped, "Shut the door!" He looked Erik up and down with a disdainful look and without inviting him to sit, said "There are a few things Mr. Nielsen that you need to get straight. Firstly, I am always Mr. Macleod to you, not Norman. When you come to my office you will wear a coat."

He added, "You look scruffy with that hair, and I want you to get a haircut." He then stressed that he did not condone drinking in any form and certainly there must no drinking of alcohol during the working day. He concluded by stressing that any work submitted to him must be of a high standard and that he would not tolerate any slackness.

He sat back and rudely dismissed Erik with a wave of his hand.

Erik did not move. He pulled back a chair and sat, ignoring Norman's protest that he had not invited him to do so. Erik, not the least intimidated, softly said, "Norman, you have not heard my side. Firstly, in the outside office, I agree, I will always call you Mr. MacLeod in front of staff. However, when it is just you and me in here, I will call you Norman and I expect you to call me Erik as it should be with a cordial working relationship. Secondly, you should also know that I only wear a coat in winter and my hair is my own, I won't be getting a haircut. You won't have to worry about drinking as I never drink during the working week."

Erik went on to say that he was good at what he did, and he doubted Norman would have any concerns in that regard.

Comments not entirely unreasonable. However, they were like a red rag to a bull with Norman who never had anyone stand up to him.

As Erik stood up, Norman seething, exclaimed loudly, "Get out of here, you impertinent lout! Don't come back until you show respect!" Erik unperturbed, showed no emotion as he sat down again. He leant forward and in his forthright manner said, "Mister MacLeod, you have a reputation as a mean, cantankerous bastard. I have never worked with you, but, man to man, I am prepared to judge you for myself. We need to work together and to do this properly, we need to treat one another in a respectful way. Sure, if I stuff up, I expect a kick in the backside, but I don't think there will be much need. So, let's do it right."

Norman blood red in the face now, exploded in a loud voice, "You can't talk to me like that." Erik outwardly calm and seemingly unconcerned, replied, "No Norman, that was not unreasonable in attempting to set things straight between us."

Norman lost all control and sense of proportion, standing up he snarled at Erik through clenched teeth, "You are totally insubordinate and guilty of misconduct, you impertinent lout. I am going to the Deputy Managing Director who is a friend, to have you sacked."

Erik was taken aback by the man's vehemence and over-the-top reaction. With Norman breaking into a winning smirk, Erik shook his head and grinned. Surprised, Norman's smirk turned to a frown as Erik informed him, "You might have the Deputy Managing Director on your side mate, but the President and long-time member of my Surf Club is the Bank's Chairman. He and I are on close, friendly terms."

He did not have to rub it in, but did anyway, saying, "I don't think it is me that has to be concerned Norman if I pass the word!" A riposte that made Norman think and worry. He forgot about any sacking.

Erik walked around to the Southern Division area and called the staff together. He introduced himself and expressed the hope that they would work well as a team. He stressed he was a fair man and would support them as far as he could, looking in return for transparency in all their dealings. There was a half-hearted, unenthused response. When he finished talking, the group as one, turned their backs and returned to their desks.

They were certainly a very unhappy and disgruntled group. Over the next couple of days, Erik invited each of them into his office for a talk. He asked about their personal background and their work in the Division. It soon became clear that morale was at rock bottom.

They had been bullied and ground down over a long time by the constant negativity deriving from ongoing, petty criticism and increasing demands for greater attention to detail. There was never a comment about a job well done. There was no camaraderie nor team spirit. In the staff's defensive response to try and cover every aspect, they were drafting long memoranda to support their recommendations.

Within the Division, there were four teams processing applications applicable to each type of loan (home, small business, rural and corporate). These were headed by a senior experienced Team Leader who held an approval discretion covering most applications received.

Applications more than their authority were submitted to Erik who approved or submitted them further up the line to the Divisional Group Leader, State Managers or to the Credit Committee of the Board for consideration.

It was Erik's responsibility, subject to Norman's overview, to manage the general running of the Division on a day-to-day basis and ensure it operated effectively. It was up to him then to talk to the Team Leaders and tell them that the Division needed to lift its game and reduce the time taken to decide the fate of applications.

Comments regarding the merits or otherwise of individual applications should in future be brief and to the point. There were to be no more long memoranda attempting to justify recommendations.

The Team Leaders were horrified and objected strongly, "Norman will have a fit and come down on us hard. He will rave and rant, it's just not worth it!" Erik told them, "Just pass the word and leave Norman to me." As they departed, one of them remarked, "Good luck mate, you are going to need it."

A couple of days later before he had had an opportunity to front Norman, Erik noticed Lorna Jones, a member of the housing loan team scurrying past his office, crying and obviously distressed. He got her into his office and asked what was wrong. Through sobs, she explained that she had just come from Mr. MacLeod's office where she had received a traumatic dressing down about a recent loan approval she had processed. She had tried to rebut his criticism, but he had yelled at her, "You should not be in loans, you are a fool. Just get out of here!"

The girl was distraught and seemed to be getting worse as she talked to him. Erik rang through to Therese Briden, the Human Resources Officer and got her to come round and try to console her.

About an hour later, Therese Briden returned to his office and closed the door. She told Erik that Lorna had remained upset and could not be consoled. She had arranged for a bank car to take her home. Therese then told Erik that whilst the dressing down must have been bad enough, she had suspected that there was something else more distressing to upset her.

On further probing it had all come out. Lorna had confided that she believed Norman McLeod had again tried to look up her skirt dropping his pen on the floor and getting down on his hands and knees under the desk. This was not the first time it had happened, and she had been too scared to speak out previously. Lorna had added that the girl from the section who had recently resigned had been a friend of hers and she had confided that she too had had a similar experience.

Therese said that in the light of this, she thought it best to get Lorna out of the Division straight away. Erik agreed. But then there was the question of Norman.

Therese said that despite her entreaties, Lorna was frightened and was not prepared to make a formal complaint. Without this, any accusation was only hearsay, and they would have to be careful in how they went about it. Nevertheless, something had to be done!

Erik said, "Leave the bastard to me."

Before fronting Norman, Erik talked to the Housing Loan Leader and asked why Norman had carpeted the loans girl when it was, he who approved the loan. The Team Leader replied, "That's his style. Each day he gets the approvals for the previous day from one of the teams and goes through each file with a fine-tooth comb. He won't front any of the Team Leaders (although he gave poor old Stan Thompson hell) but takes sadistic pleasure in ripping the kids to shreds but mostly the girls!"

Erik said to the Team Leader give me the file Lorna Jones was involved with. When he got it, he went to his office and studied it closely. He found nothing wrong with the processing so, he wondered, what was the who-ha all about.

Norman's office door was closed but Erik barged in without knocking. Norman had been lying back in his office chair with his feet on the desk dozing. He was rudely awakened and took a moment or two to recover his composure. When he did, he snarled angrily at Erik demanding to know why he had barged in unceremoniously.

Erik ignored him and slammed the door. Sitting down, he demanded tersely why Lorna Jones was given a dressing down. Norman now himself, responded loftily "Because, she did not do her job properly, that's why!" When Erik produced the file and said, "I have examined her processing, I can't see it." Norman laughed sarcastically, saying, "Then, you aren't much good either, are you?"

Norman then raised specific omissions in her checking such as no confirmation of applicants' taxation position, nor confirmation of existing loan commitments. Importantly too, there was also an incorrect calculation of the applicants' repayment capacity.

Erik shook his head and calmly refuted each of these three criticisms in turn.

As to the taxation query, both applicants were on payroll (pay slips were on file) and their accounts showed no evidence of other income such as dividends or rental receipts. No shares or investment properties were disclosed in their application. Taxation was deducted on PAYG and the need to confirm their position was certainly not warranted.

Erik pointed out that commitments shown on their credit reference report were over five years old and Lorna has checked with applicants that these were no longer current. Again, there was no evidence of any regular outward payments showing on their cheque account indicative of other commitments.

Erik finally pointed out to Norman that whilst their application showed one dependant, the record of interview on file mentioned that this person, a 22-year-old daughter who had just completed university was moving out of the family home to take up a job in Canberra within the month. Erik took delight in pointing out to Norman that he had missed this and that the living allowance estimate used to assess repayment capacity based on two people and not three, was correct. There was, indeed, no substance to any of his criticisms.

Before Norman could respond, Erik took him to task for his humiliating bullying of Lorna, stressing that you can't treat people like that. He concluded, by telling him, "I don't want you ever again to confront any of our staff unless I am present."

Norman brushed aside his behaviour at the interview with a wave of his hands, retorting, "It was only words." Then bending forward a little, he smiled nastily and added, "Well and how do you think you are going to make me stop doing what I like, you lout? You forget, I am the Group Leader, I do what I want."

Erik sighed heavily and baiting him, replied, "Yes, you bloody old hypocrite, like getting down under your desk to look up the skirts of young women you have called into your office on pretext."

Norman looked at Erik aghast! The shot had obviously hit home. He had visibly blanched. But, he exploded, "How dare you say such a thing. That's preposterous! You have gone too far."

Erik replied, "You know what the truth is Norman" and bluffing, added, "The girls are considering accusing you formally. Right or wrong, if that happens you are finished. Your reputation will be tarnished forever. So, you better behave, or you will go down the drain."

Norman obviously distressed now, blurted out, "That's blackmail!" To which Erik replied, "You better believe it" and with that marched out of the office with his fingers crossed. But it worked.

Erik passed the word that individual staff should not engage in discussions with Norman unless he was present.

Erik further pre-empted matters by personally reviewing the daily approval files submitted to Norman. Beneath each approval he affixed the following signed certificate:

I HAVE REVIEWED THIS LOAN APPROVAL
PROCESSING HAS FOLLOWED CORRECT GUIDELINES
DECISION TO APPROVE IS SUPPORTED

Subsequently, Norman was too intimidated to confront Erik about any perceived deficiencies. He persevered for a couple of months with his daily review but then gave it away, directing the Admin's internal auditor to make sample checks in his stead.

Norman now rarely left his office and left Erik alone to run the place. He had no reason for complaint in that regard. With Norman off their back, the decision time to approve applications came back into line with the other divisions. Simon's ploy had worked.

Whilst individuals within the group seemed happy enough, Erik perceived that there was no sense of belonging nor cohesion.

Within a few weeks of all this happening, it was Christmas Eve. It was normal practice for the whole office to knock off for the holidays at lunch time with each Group Leader sitting down and enjoying lunch with his staff.

Not so in Southern Division. Whilst staff downed tools at lunchtime, there was no lunch together and not even any Christmas well-wishes from Norman. Erik resolved that it would be different this year. When he approached Norman, he was, as expected, peremptorily rebuffed. He then went and obtained Simon Sinclair's authorisation to buy lunch for his staff.

And so, on the day having finished work, they sat at their desks and enjoyed the Chinese takeaway Erik had arranged. Norman did not make an appearance. There was no alcohol, only soft drinks. This was Erik's own call and not due to any influence of Norman's. Perhaps because of this, things were flat with little talk amongst the group about Christmas and the holiday break.

Erik was thinking frantically of what he could do to liven things up, when the young fellow, Tony Rossi, who had recently been transferred in from a branch to replace Lorna Jones asked deferentially whether he could do something to entertain everybody. Not knowing what to expect, Erik told him "to go for it."

Tony sat down at the front with a piano accordion he produced from somewhere. He started and everyone sat there entranced as young Tony playing like a virtuoso sang a medley of well-known Italian songs in a beautiful tenor voice. When he finished, everybody went crazy, clapping and screaming for more. He continued with old favourites and then Christmas carols with everybody joining in and singing together. Erik noted that three of his young men had stood up together at the back, all singing, with their arms around each other's shoulders. "That's a promising" he thought.

At 3.30pm, as Simon Sinclair had directed for the whole office, he called, "Lets close it down kids, it's time to go home." There were cries of disappointment, but these stopped when Tony stood up and started playing the South Sydney Rugby League team song, which starts off "Glory, Glory to South Sydney" but instead of singing "South Sydney" he substituted "Glory, Glory to South Divey" which worked in well.

But there was more, after the "Glory, glory to South Divey" three times and a final line of "South Divey marches on" he sang:

"We're heads above the northies*
And the westies*too
We are the cock on the top of the clock
So, cockadoodledo."

(* the other lending divisions)

He continued with two more verses ending up with the "Glory, Glory to South Divey":

"Erik is our leader.
A bloke who is true blue
He brought us altogether.
So, cockadoodledo.

We were you know a motley lot.
A much-divided crew
But Erik's nous has set us right.
So, cockadoodledo."

The kids went wild, and they all joined in together singing the Glory, Glory chorus. Sing it again they all called and as they sang, they all teamed up with the three young fellows at the back, until the whole staff complement stood in a half circle side by side arms around shoulders singing "their team song". Erik thought to himself. "My God, it's happening. They are coming together!"

There was one other verse concerning "Norman who is a law man" which Erik banned from ever being sung again.

Simon Sinclair and Flite, attracted by the boisterous singing and the loud "cockadoodledos" came into the Division area and stood alongside Erik. Giving him the thumbs up, Simon exclaimed, "This is absolutely wonderful Erik. Looks like you have got yourself a real team."

And he had. Thanks, in no small way to Tony, his accordion and some spontaneous ad-libbing. Young Tony was mobbed and enthusiastically thanked by them all but particularly by Erik.

The cockadoodledo was henceforth the exuberant "rebel" cry of Southern Division staff. It signalled that the reign of the ogre was over.

TEDDY AGAIN

An Impetuous Man

Teddy was head over heels in love with Trish.

They had been living together for a couple of years and were mixing in a social set that consisted of his school friends and Gordon rugby mates. They got on well, had similar values and there was an unspoken expectation that down the track they would marry and start a family.

It didn't happen suddenly, but Teddy noticed that Trish had started to lose her ardour. Nothing he could put his finger on, but he felt it just the same. Then there were occasions she did not come home for the night phoning him to explain that a big story was breaking, and she was staying at work to cover it. There was, however, nothing extraordinary in the news the next day.

One evening when she got home at 11.30pm, he confronted her as it was readily apparent that there was someone else.

Trish broke down in tears. She was sorry, she didn't mean it to happen, but she had fallen in love with the TV station's star presenter. She told Teddy he was a good man who had everything going for him, but her new man was exciting and had promised to push her in her career. She did not mention that he had a beautiful home at Dover Heights looking down on to the harbour, a chocolate brown jaguar and a big yacht moored at Rushcutters Bay.

She packed, called a cab, kissed him on the forehead and saying "Sorry Teddy" left.

Teddy was shell-shocked. He just could not believe it. He had a couple of scotches and lay down on the bed sad and disappointed. He really loved the woman and had thought it was forever.

His world was shattered.

Next morning, very depressed he went to work. It was not good, Charles kept nagging him about completion of the branch quarterly business and statistical return due the following Wednesday.

Today was Friday, Monday was a public holiday and Charles wanted it on his desk first thing Tuesday so he would have ample time to check it.

It was not going to be a good day!

Teddy put his head down and got into it, thankful at least he had something to distract him from his heartbreak.

At midday, Charles came out of his office to tell Teddy he was going home for lunch. Normally, before he left, he would ask the teller whether he was running short of any notes and needed a top-up from treasury. Today he didn't.

About a quarter of an hour later the teller called to Teddy that he had had a run on his twenties and asked whether he might get $4,000 from Treasury. Charles and Teddy were joint custodians. Teddy crankily asked the teller why in God's name had he not raised it before, adding that there was no way they could access Treasury until Charles returned. The teller apologised weakly but explained he really needed the twenties soon. It was payday for Henri's staff and every week on Fridays they came in to draw their pay.

Before anybody could say any more through the front door came the retired Chairman's wife wanting to withdraw $200 from her savings account in new $20 notes.

That settled things. Teddy ushered her into Charles' office and sat her down explaining that Charles was at lunch, and he needed to get the new notes that she always obtained from the safe.

Hoping against hope, he then opened the top drawer of Charles' desk and there, thank God, were his keys.

Teddy went to the safe and with Charles' key took two 100-piece packets of new $20 notes. He made the entries in the Treasury Register, got the teller to sign for the cash and initialled as senior custodian in a facsimile of Charles' initial.

He sat back in his office. He had done the wrong thing; he had been stupid! The heartbreak of Trish leaving was also crushing him.

He regressed and started to feel cornered like when he was in trouble at school and climbed up on the roof. He snapped, saying to himself "I have had this! I am getting out."

He went back to the Treasury compartment and took all the $50 and $100 note bundles amounting to $50,000 and put them in a satchel. He left the remaining twenties, tens and fives amounting to $40,000 as there were too many bundles to handle conveniently. He locked the compartment and put the keys back in Charles' desk drawer.

When everybody else left the office that afternoon, Teddy set the alarm, locked the front door and drove home.

He was wearing a business suit. He threw a couple of shirts and a couple of changes of casual wear in a carry-all, grabbed his passport and got a cab to the airport. There he bought a ticket to Johannesburg and flew out that evening on the South African Airlines flight. Why South Africa, he could not tell you. It just seemed right at the time. The fact that there was a plane leaving Australia within a few hours though, must have had some relevance.

Before he left, he telephoned his mother telling her about his breakup with Trish and that he was going away for a while to start afresh. He mailed her his car keys.

When he arrived in Joburg, he booked into a comfortable inexpensive hotel and started to explore his surroundings. He did the tourist thing for three days looking around the city and surrounds. At the time, South Africa was in the grip of apartheid, an authoritarian political culture based on white supremacy enabling the minority white population to dominate the country politically, socially, and economically.

Teddy did not like what he saw, the harsh draconian segregation of races such as the notices insisting specific facilities were for white person use only, that black people could not own businesses in white areas, the pass system and that trains, buses, ambulances and hospitals were segregated.

He noted that there were attractive non-white women, and he was dumbfounded when he learned that it was a criminal offence for him to enter a relationship with them or even to fraternise socially.

He started looking for a job. Although white, he was not South African, and employers were reluctant to hire outsiders. After a couple of weeks though, he talked his way into employment with a wine merchant exporting local wine. All staff were white, and Teddy started to pick up the threads of local culture and how to conduct himself when he encountered black people.

It certainly was hugely different.

He opened a bank account and deposited his $50,000 without difficulty on production of his passport.

He continued to live at the hotel and was hesitant to leave it of an evening on the advice of the Indian doorman. With nothing to do he gravitated to the bar and talked to Benji, the South African born Japanese bar tender. Benji had a degree from London University in Geology. In one of the few exceptions to the rigid demarcation of races under apartheid, Japanese people had been granted "honorary white" status (the Government not wishing to offend the big Japanese cartels and jeopardise lucrative trade arrangements).

Whilst this in theory afforded Benji the same general freedom as a white person, when it came down to employment at a management level he was "non-white". He had thought that with his degree he would gain employment with one of the big mining companies, but it was a vain hope. After several unsuccessful applications and unfriendly interviews, he gave up.

After a few weeks, Teddy and Benji became friendly and open with one another. Teddy was not happy in his job, and he realised he would never get rich working there. One evening, he asked Benji "What have you got to do here to become rich?"

Benji laughed and replied, "Best way I guess is to rob banks!"

Teddy laughed, muttering "Done that! What else?" Benji went on to explain that a few people were still getting rich by freelance prospecting for gold and diamonds.

South Africa, of course, was one of the world's leading producers of both gold and diamonds with big mining concerns at the forefront in bringing this about. Nevertheless, there were still pockets of country that had not been tested and smaller prospectors were trying their luck there. Obviously not all were striking it rich, but a few had made big finds.

A couple of nights later, Teddy put it to Benji, "Look, I have enough money to last us for 12 months or so, what about you and me going partners and start prospecting. We will go halves, equally, in whatever we find." Benji did not take long to make up his mind. Next evening, he told Teddy, "I'm in!"

For a couple of days, they researched Government geological data, industry reports and anything relating to diamond and gold prospecting. After much soul searching, they decided they would look for alluvial diamonds in the beds of ancient water courses.

One area that appealed to Benji was in the northwest of Lesotho, a separate country, totally landlocked within the borders of South Africa. Diamond mines there in the country's Maluti Mountains, 11,000 feet above sea level, were known for producing big high-quality gems that fetched considerably higher prices. The area though was very remote and undeveloped.

Teddy bought an old Land Rover and they drove off to Lesotho some 450kms away. A long tiring drive. They arrived at Maseru, the capital just inside the border.

The next day they chartered a Cessna and directed the pilot to fly over the mountains looking for likely spots for prospecting. In the middle of the country near a place called Thaba Tsera in very rough mountain terrain they came to the Orange River and perceived a stretch where it had changed direction. The old riverbed lay about 50 yards away from its current bank. It looked very promising and seemingly could be accessed by four-wheel drive.

They spent the next week preparing, acquiring prospecting gear like pans, sieves, and a sluice as well as a petrol generator and camping equipment. They were warned that even in summer, it could be very cold often with snow, and they made sure that they would be well rugged up and warm.

While Lesotho is generally regarded as safe, people are poor and there is a high crime rate. They bought themselves a couple of Springfield hunting rifles and ample ammunition just in case they encountered trouble.

They spent another week seeking the necessary government approvals to prospect in the area they proposed.

When they were all set and loaded up, they took off for the site.

Getting to Taha Tsera from Maseru is not easy. The drive takes some 6 hours over precipitous and rough mountain roads, crossing high mountain passes and winding past remote highland villages.

The Range Rover coped well, their tyres were nearly new, and they experienced little difficulty in arriving at Taha Tsera. They passed through the town and continued along the road until they could see the river below them to their right.

They turned off the road such as it was and very gingerly descended. It turned out to be not too bad and at the bottom they followed the river until they came to their proposed prospecting site.

Diamonds had been discovered in the area thirty years previously. While some commercial mining had been tried, these attempts had been abandoned due to the remoteness of the area and its then ongoing political volatility. The political situation had subsequently eased, and government was now stable.

Similarly, sole prospectors had also been deterred by its isolation and only a handful had ever tried their luck. Teddy and Benji were proposing to prospect on a site that had never been explored before.

Pumping river water through the alluvial debris from the fissures and crevices in the dry riverbed, they slowly accumulated some good quality small stones. It was hard work and living tough and they began to wonder was it all worth it. On their reckoning, after two years efforts, their hoard was probably worth at best $100,000. Nevertheless, they decided to stick it out for a couple more years.

Some 6 months later, their luck changed somewhat when they found in their wash a couple of 30 carat stones side by side. They continued to regularly find small high-quality stones. Occasionally, bigger stones turned up in their wash but never a Kohinoor crown jewel.

They were working mostly five days a week and resting on weekends. They ate reasonably well, eating a lot of the prevalent Smallmouth Yellowfish from the river, Boerewors sausage, tinned stuff and vegetables bought from the local village Sani people. They stuck to it though for four years with occasional wild R and R stays in Joburg loving the hot water, cold beer, good steak, fresh fruit, soft beds, good whisky and bad women.

They got on well and even though living close together they never squabbled. Benji's calmness (and regular periods of meditation) rubbed off on Teddy. Even though they were living rough, he came to realise he was content, even happy.

They were only threatened physically once when three would-be robbers coming down the river and attracted by their campfire beached their boat and started for their tent armed with machetes.

The boys were asleep but were awakened by their bull mastiff Jo Jo's growl. The dog rushed out of the tent and grabbed the nearest intruder by the top of his thigh. The man screamed and his two mates ran to him. The boys grabbed their guns and followed Jo Jo.

One ran at Benji with a raised machete. Benji shot him cold.

The other two, pursued by Jo Jo, turned and ran for their boat. Benji shot them as they started to push their boat away from the riverbank. The river carried their boat and bodies away. Benji dragged the other body to the water's edge and let it go.

Teddy was surprised at Benji's sang froid in killing three individuals and coolly disposing of their bodies. Benji explained that the men were not locals, probably Swahili from the north, "bad buggers". Violence towards isolated people was commonplace and that three bodies were found floating down the river would not arouse any curiosity. He pointed out that the individuals in question would have had no compunction in killing them as they slept, and they might well have done so if it had not been for Jo Jo. So, it was best there were no survivors otherwise they would inevitably receive a return revenge attack by a stronger party.

After this incident, they hid their growing collection some 50 yards away from their campsite under a large river boulder right up against the escarpment. They were in a quandary though what to do next.

One Sunday afternoon at the local hotel where they had gone for the weekend, they met an old German with long white hair drinking

Schnapps and listening to Beethoven on a battered CD player. He turned out to be a retired geologist who had married a local girl years earlier.

When she died, he found he was attached to the place and could not leave. Now, he just loved roaming the mountains, doing a little prospecting and a bit of diamond cutting on the side. He had struck it rich years ago. Living was cheap, no hassles and so he had decided to end his days here. He lived with two young local Sani girls.

The boys talked to him about what they had been doing and Hans took a shine to them. They subsequently met him regularly and got to know him well. Seeking his advice, he said it was better to get stones cut before they tried to sell them. He told them he had always cut his own stones and was expert at it. He offered to cut theirs.

Still a bit wary, they took their hoard of uncut stones to him a few at a time, smaller ones first. He was obviously expert, and the finished product was invariably beautifully done. Hans was impressed with their larger stones which he said would bring big money.

He also advised them not to sell in South Africa because brokers there would fleece them. He recommended a German broking firm in Switzerland. He also advised them not to take less than $500,000 US dollars for the lot as it was worth more than that. He would not take money for cutting their stones. He was delighted though when they bought him a couple of cases of single malt scotch whisky.

What really put the icing on the cake, however, was their gift of the latest CD audio player plus boxed sets of Beethoven, Bach, Brahms, and Schuman.

Talking previously to a broker in Taha Tsera and working on figures he had mentioned, the boys thought they had best part of $400,000 but no more. Hans' estimate was certainly welcome.

They agreed after four years rough work whatever they had was enough. And so, after giving Hans Jo Jo and signing their mining lease over to him, they drove to Johannesburg and took a Swiss Air flight to Zurich.

When they arrived at the broker's office recommended by Hans they were led to a plush office and served a glass of schnapps. Within a minute or two a very precise-looking thin, gaunt man came into the office and welcomed them warmly. He introduced himself as Max. He had only one hand.

Hans had already foreshadowed their arrival. It came out in following discussion that he and Max had grown up together and had been in the German army in World War 2 serving together on the Russian front.

They had been captured just inside the Polish border after the Russian breakout from Leningrad but had escaped by climbing through a hole that Hans had punched in the rusted iron roof of their cattle truck and jumping off into the snow.

They were hardly any better off, starving, and frozen, trudging exhausted, westward along the railway line. In a few hours, it would have been the end for them, a lonely death in the snow. Max was making heavy weather of it and Hans had to help him negotiate the heavy snow drifts.

Fortunately for them, the German army had counter attacked in the sector and more by luck than good management had broken the Russian lines. They were picked up by forward elements and sent to the rear.

Both were suffering badly from frost bite, Max losing a hand from holding his great coat together to protect his chest from the cold. They never returned to the Front again convalescing in a small South Western German town until the war ended. They then went their separate ways but kept in touch over the years bound together by all they had been through.

Hans had told Max they were good young men and asked that he give them a fair deal with their diamonds. He did particularly, as he said, the stones were high quality and had been expertly cut. They could not believe it when an amount of $580,000 US dollars was paid into their joint Swiss bank account (on the exchange rate at that time nearly

$900,000 Australian dollars). Certainly, a worthwhile reward for four years hard slog.

They had indeed been lucky and done much better than most. They had been fortunate to have selected an area which in years to come would become a very lucrative field for the big corporate miners.

Coming into money, Benji married his long-time South African born Japanese sweetheart in Johannesburg, the reception being held in Benji's parents' restaurant. Teddy was his best man.

Teddy's parents had died 12 months apart, two years ago. He was now very wealthy. His parents' home facing directly across New South Head Road from the harbour had sold for more than $2 million. The share portfolio was worth over a million.

He roamed for a while doing all the tourist things, going on safari, visiting Kruger National Park, Victoria Falls, the Kalahari. He flew to Egypt and toured the Pyramids and historic sites and sailed down the Nile.

But he was now pining for home.

Taking the horse by the bridle, he decided to telephone the ABC Bank's Head Office and spoke to the Human Resources Inspector. He confirmed that yes, he had stolen $50,000 a few years back but if he repaid now say $60,000 could he be assured the Bank would not initiate legal proceedings against him. He stressed he wanted very much to return home but was fearful that he might have to face the consequences of his earlier action.

When he contacted the Inspector again, he was assured that a deal was possible but, the amount missing was not $50,000 but $90,000. If he paid $110,000, he would receive the necessary written assurance of waiver.

Teddy flopped back in his chair, momentarily flummoxed, realising immediately that Charles, the old pompous bugger, had grasped the opportunity to get his hands on the residual $40,000 and let him carry the blame for the full $90,000 theft.

Recovering, he told the Inspector he was agreeable and then talked through with him details of his settlement payment and the format of the waiver letter.

Before concluding the discussion, he asked the Staff Inspector whether he knew what had happened to Charles Cooper who by now should have well and truly retired. The Inspector told him that Charles had retired soon after the theft and had been reprimanded for his negligence in not safeguarding his security keys. He went on to say Charles and his wife had gone back to England to be with their son. He understood Charles had recently died in Cornwall.

Teddy repaid his debt to the bank and returned soon afterwards to Australia. There were no repercussions. As soon as he could, he called on the family solicitors to discuss his affairs. He had not used any of the sale proceeds of his parent's home which had been placed on bank term deposit (but understandably with a Bank other than the ABC).

When their talk was concluding, the solicitor handed him a letter from Charles Cooper.

In it, Charles told Teddy that when he discovered the theft, he was very angry not the least of which being his disappointment at Teddy's abuse of trust and not doing the right thing. On a spur of the moment whim to get back at him, Charles removed the residual $40,000 in smaller notes and reported that the theft involved the total $90,000.

He took the cash home. He did not need it and he became concerned about what to do with it. Finally, he donated it to the rebuilt St. Hildegard's Orphanage in Berlin that his Lancaster had inadvertently destroyed during the war.

Charles went on to say, "Reflecting on things further and knowing my life will be coming to an end shortly, I came to the realisation that I had done you wrong by letting you take the blame for the full amount of the theft. Accordingly, I now enclose my cheque for $40,000 payable to salve my conscience of this misdeed."

Teddy, of course, was well and truly taken aback and thought to himself, "the old bugger, dinki di and upright to the last."

Charles had died some 12 months earlier and his estate Teddy knew, would have been finalised. He never presented the cheque knowing it would only open fresh wounds and cause unhappiness to Penelope and her son.

He left Sydney and moved to Noosa on the Sunshine Coast. He persuaded Benji and his new Japanese wife to join him.

They started a Japanese seafood restaurant on the Noosa River with exquisite Japanese décor and a beautiful koi pool. Benji's family who owned a restaurant in Joburg came to take care of the culinary side of things. Benji had claimed they were expert in the art of Japanese cuisine and Teddy had accepted that this was the case. They proved to be all Benji claimed and in a very short time the Nishi-ki-goi (the name of a beautiful koi fish) became to be regarded as one of the best and most exclusive restaurants in Noosa (which touted itself as one of Australia's prime spots for fine dining).

Teddy had been involved in a couple of relationships since locating on the Sunshine Coat but had never found "the one". Benji and his family kept on him to find a nice lady and settle down. After one occasion when Benji's mother had maternally berated him thus he wondered what Trish, the woman with whom he was in love with years before, was doing. Watching local television one Monday evening when the restaurant was closed, there she was, still very presentable, reading the news.

Even then, he procrastinated but after one further lecture from Benji's mother he plucked up his courage and tried to contact her.

Nothing!!!!!!

Some days later, he received a querulous voice mail message asking "Is that really you, Teddy? Where are you? What are you doing? Please call me, Trish."

He did. Trish had been away on an assignment and having received the message from the station (without his name) assumed it was work related and ignored it. Having got back to the station she had seen his name and called him back. She was delighted to hear from him. Her relationship with the star presenter had not lasted. She had come to realise that he was a "show pony" with a lot of front and charm and a huge ego but not much else. He did, however, help her career-wise and she was grateful for that. When she discovered he had been cheating on her, she left him and spent two years in London working on British Television. She had been working for the past 12 months or so as a news presenter at a Brisbane television station.

Teddy briefly recounted all that had happened to him but without mentioning Benji and their diamond success. When Teddy enquired was there any reason why he could not come down to Brisbane to meet her, she giggled and declared "she was fancy free and on the lookout for a nice man."

They met and it was like a bonfire. Their mutual attraction was spontaneous.

They found they got along well as before with Trish repeatedly telling Teddy how happy she was that he had found her again. They became lovers but did not live together, their jobs of necessity keeping them apart.

Benji's mother again intervened and berated them both on their arrangement. One way or the other, the pair of you should get together.

For Teddy, the restaurant was little more than something to keep him busy. He was starting to get interested in the possibility of a new career. Benji's mother's nagging eventually prevailed. He told Benji he and his family could keep the Nishi-ki-goi as he was going to live in Brisbane with Trish. He did! He also went back to University and finished his law degree. He subsequently gained entrance to the bar and quickly made a name for himself defending criminals, particularly those allegedly guilty of financial fraud.

Teddy and Trish married and lived happily together regularly visiting Noosa to catch up with Benji and his growing family. Teddy and Benji remained firm close friends for the rest of their lives.

At times, Teddy would reflect on the past and would think about Charles and recall how honourable the man was. He greatly regretted how on the spur of a moment, he had stupidly done the man wrong and set himself off on a wild chase that, fortunately, turned out well.

NISHI-KI-GOI

Source: Taro Kodama (undated)
"What is the history of nishi-ki-goi"
www.Kodamakoifarm.com

The name, "Nishi ki goi" emerged some hundreds of years ago in Niigata prefecture in Japan when the fish were developed by farmers seeking a consistent food source that could survive harsh winters. The result was a beautifully coloured fish with a fine form.

Koi is a Japanese language homophone for "affection" or "love" and the fish are universally perceived there as living symbols of love and friendship.

As a result of their attractiveness and symbolic connotation the keeping of these fish in outdoor pools and water gardens particularly by the noble class has been popular in Japan for centuries.

When people feed the koi with "Fu" a special food made for them from wheat gluten, the koi calmly come to the surface to feed not displaying any greed or aggression to others. This characteristic is often pointed out to children as a value that they should follow.

Nishi-ki-goi, are indeed vibrant "living jewels" and objects of natural wonder.

THE CALABRIAN MEN

Bruno's father had been taken prisoner by Australian troops in 1941 during World War 2 following their capture of Italian-held Bardia in Libya. He and many other Italian prisoners of war spent the rest of the war working on Australian farms. He and many of his fellow POWs liked Australia and after repatriation home, they migrated back with their wives and families.

Many of them settled in the Riverina region of New South Wales where their farming expertise with grapes and citrus was very welcome. With hard work, shrewd buying and some clandestine dealings Bruno's father died a very wealthy man.

Bruno carried on after his father died and he and his brother became even more prosperous owning a major share in a national brand winery, orchards and a popular restaurant in Bana Street, the main thoroughfare of Griffith, the major centre in the Riverina.

Bruno was the acknowledged leader of the Italian community, a role which by repute probably also meant, he was the senior local Mafia Don, the boss of all the bosses! He was very generous in support of the local community, his parish church, the aged Italian people's home, the local soccer team. He was an avid bocce player.

Nonetheless, his reputation went before him, particularly his strongly rumoured association with the production and supply of drugs. He was also linked with but never convicted of involvement with the regular violence endemic in the drug trade.

The family group banked with the local branch of the ABC Bank although their $2 million line of credit facility was controlled by the Bank's NSW

Administration, specifically Norman MacLeod in charge of Southern Division.

Bruno did not like paying his bills and the group's account was always in arrears. The account was constantly coming across Norman's desk for dilatory payment, and he lost patience with the continuing delinquency. He peremptorily demanded Bruno come to Sydney to discuss the operation of the account.

Bruno bristled at the tone of the request and came up with his accountant, his solicitor and body-guard ready for a fight.

The Bank was well secured by mortgage over the Group's real estate and an equitable charge over other assets such as wine stocks. Whilst they were "late payers" they always met their commitment eventually. The Group's accountant tabled up-to-date financial statements confirming they were operating profitably.

Bruno opened by telling Norman angrily that the Bank was not at risk so what was he going on about. In return, Norman told Bruno tersely that he must meet repayments on time otherwise he would raise the interest rate to cover "excessive administrative costs."

They sat there for a minute or two in silence, glaring at one another. Then Bruno got up, banged his fist on the table and said to Norman "I don't like the way you talk. You show no respect. You don't know whom you are dealing with. I have great sway with my people. So, be careful compagno! Tread carefully!"

With that, he turned, and he and his entourage left the building.

Norman just sat there dumbfounded, his pomposity in tatters. Then remembering one of his staff had been taking notes, he threatened the young fellow about mentioning any word of happenings adding that he would draft the diary note of the interview for the file.

The subsequent diary notes briefly mentioned that the Group was continuing to trade profitably and whilst they were sometimes slow in meeting repayments the Bank was not at risk. A complete whitewash!

Some days after the interview, the account was brought back into order from sale of "blending" wine stock and future repayments were always made on time. So, while feathers had been ruffled on both sides, a good result for the Bank had been achieved.

Norman let everybody know that it was his firm approach that achieved this outcome. Nonetheless, he was still cranky within himself.

A few days after this incident, he received a call from the Manager of his Liverpool branch seeking favourable consideration for a loan of $300,000 for two older Italian men to buy land for a market garden. They had been knocked back elsewhere and were well short of security. However, a leading businessman from Griffith, a substantial client apparently known to management was prepared to guarantee them and put up the necessary security.

As fate would have it, the businessman in question was none other than our Bruno who just a few days before had upset Norman. On learning this, Norman threw a tantrum and notwithstanding his concocted diary note of amicable discussion reiterated he was not prepared to enter talks with any more Italians.

So, by default it fell to Flite to conduct the interview with the two applicants and the Manager Liverpool.

The two Italian applicants, Lennie, and Joe were small sun-wrinkled men in their forties. They had come to Australia some ten years earlier with their families to work for Bruno. They had served him well and had saved enough for the deposit on the proposed market garden land.

Bruno knew his men and was obviously very certain they would not fail him. He readily agreed to guarantee them.

Bruno, particularly in the light of Norman's recent diary note of interview, had to be considered a good risk for the amount. He promised to lodge sufficient property security to make up the brothers' shortfall.

The only real risk was the applicants' ability to make a go of the venture. They had had, however, many years of farm work behind them and were knowledgeable about growing vegetables, particularly tomatoes. Flite concluded that it was a reasonable business risk to back the men and approved the loan. The two were ecstatic and thankful.

As he had approved the loan, it remained under his control. In these circumstances, Flite continued to keep an eye on progress undertaking an occasional inspection. On those occasions, the brothers invited him to have a grappa or two with them. Over time, they developed a close acquaintance.

Even so, Flite remained careful to maintain an arm's length relationship and to take care that he was not compromised. It is a banking axiom, that you should never get too close. You never know where it might lead.

It was evident from Flite's overview that the market garden was well managed and showed every indication of prosperity. The place was a picture! Tomatoes were growing beautifully in groves. A dam had been built and an irrigation system watering every plant on the site had been set up.

The old broken-down fibro house on the land had been added on to, it had a new tin roof and was freshly painted.

A second "removal" house had been brought on site to accommodate everybody and a big, corrugated iron packing shed erected. There was a neat garden around the houses with pencil pines reminiscent of "the old country".

The brothers were going well financially never missing a repayment on their loan. In fact, they had started making repayments more than the contractual amount even before income from tomatoes came on stream.

Twelve months after funding they had paid off half their debt. The flow of money into the account was well more than that estimated in their budget. When queried, it was explained that the family women had started their own business producing tomato sauce from bruised and damaged fruit. It had become popular being sold in delicatessens in Italian areas such as Leichhardt and in up market charcuteries in Double Bay and Woollahra. The ingredients included salt, garlic, chilli, and a secret spice that made it special. When queried as to what it was, the women just giggled and shook their heads.

Flite had reservations about this explanation. There had to be some other income source to generate this much cash. When queried further, Lennie and Joe just shrugged, shook their heads and kept repeating "Just the farm! Just the tomatoes!".

Things had been going well but started to go wrong when an aggressive rival competitor tried to muscle in on Bruno's criminal turf. Violence erupted and the brothers left their farm to return to Griffith. In the ensuing fracas there, shots were fired into homes, a couple of Bruno's people were beaten up and two trucks firebombed. A violent response was not long coming with the execution of the Senior Don of the other gang and two of his "soldiers" in broad daylight in the car park of the Garibaldi Club in Sydney's west.

Subsequently, a truce was called and in the negotiations that followed, the residual members of the rival group considered it prudent to merge and join Bruno.

A couple of days after the execution-style killing, Lennie and Joe "went into smoke". They were nowhere to be seen and enquirers were told that they had returned to Italy on family business.

A few days later, the police raided the farm seeking Lennie and Joe whom they alleged were the "hit men" who carried out the executions on Bruno's orders. They searched the farm but found nothing.

There was a low building covered with artificial grass matting which police suspected had been used to propagate marijuana. There were marks where pots had been and heavy-duty lamps still in place but nothing that could lead to charges. The artificial grass matting was obviously intended to hide the site from air surveillance.

It was also noted that the "Due Fratelli" sauce now lacked a bit of its previous "kick"!

In Lennie and Joe's absence, the elder son of each family assumed the day to day running of the farm under their mothers' supervision.

But the boys had eyes beyond the farm. By this time, two and half years after funding, the loan had been repaid. Funds continued to pour in.

A lot of the deposits were cash, and the Bank was required to report these large transactions to AUSTRAC, the government watchdog on the lookout for laundering of "black" money or the proceeds of crime. It was recognised that the farm was a big operation. It was also common in fruit and vegetable market trading for dealings to be in cash. In these circumstances, the Bank's reports of high cash components in deposits did not arouse any undue curiosity.

The build-up in the Bank balance did not last long as the sons went ahead and acquired a disused run-down market garden of several acres. They constructed a road with kerb and guttering, street lighting and brought in power, water, and sewerage. They subdivided the block into housing lots and quickly sold them all. With the profit, they built two big houses on either side of the road into the estate which the families moved into.

With this success behind them the families became more and more focussed on subdivision development. Inevitably, the farm started to go backwards and income from this source started to decline. The families quickly recognised that they needed help to maintain their base operation. To do this, they brought out from their home village in Calabria two families who were close relatives. These people settled in quickly and it was not long before farm income returned to former levels. It was also noted that the "kick" in the tomato sauce had returned.

Among the new arrivals were two uncles who were obviously the leading farm hands. These heavily sun-wrinkled men named Tomas and Tony wore trimmed beards, their hair was grey and cut short and they continually wore dark glasses. Nonetheless, while they did look a little different, they bore a striking resemblance to Lennie and Joe. When Flite put it to them that that was who they were, they laughed and hotly denied it.

At the beginning of August this particular year, the families decided to celebrate their good fortune and life in Australia by holding a celebratory dinner on August 26 the Feast of Our Lady of Rossano, the protectress of the region in Italy where they were born.

The dinner was held in the packing shed with a long line of tables set to sit the fifty odd guests. It was bigger than "Ben Hur". Apart from family members, Bruno and Flite and their wives, there were the state and federal members, the Italian Consul, and the local Inspector of Police as well as the people the brothers did business with.

Proceedings commenced with a Franciscan friar in brown cassock and sandals accompanied by two altar boys with candles walking along the tables blessing the guests and sprinkling them with holy water. The friar then told the story of the Madonna of Rossano, of the miraculous cave there and the self- portrait of the Virgin on the cave floor. He then went on to recite a prayer of thanks to the Madonna for Her patronage and support that allowed the families to achieve prosperity and a fulfilling life.

With the conclusion of "Grace" in Italian, the festivities began.

The buffet was magnificent with every kind of Italian food imaginable many different breads and kinds of pasta, prosciutto, salamis, piazza, multiple salads and seafood. Then, there were the stands of luscious looking cakes and pastries. There was only red wine served : two varieties, Ciro the robust renowned wine of Calabria and the strong ruby red wine of Rossano.

The "three tenors" with accordion accompaniment strolled along the long table singing Italian favourites with the Italian family members and guests joining in. It was a wonderful joyous occasion.

When it seemed that most of the diners had finished eating. Bruno rose and clapped his hands twice. Immediately every Italian person stopped talking. A couple who was up at the buffet scurried back to their seats. He introduced the hosts.

Tomas and Tony (Lennie and Joe) thanked everybody for coming and again expressed thanks to the Virgin. They talked of the support they had received from many quarters and expressed their deep gratitude to those concerned. Then giving the game away completely, they singled out Flite saying that he had helped them at the very beginning when no one else would and but for him they would not be here today.

In making a presentation to him, they said they were initially at a loss to know what might be suitable. However, when they recalled his pseudonym "Flite" it all fell into place. With that they unfolded a magnificent, embroidered wall tapestry of a man with wings, with his arm across his face flying towards the sun and a city beneath him. They explained that the tapestry depicted the mythical Icarus, the first man to shake off the force of gravity and fly but who ignored advice and flew too close to the sun and his wings melted.

Responding, Flite commented that when he first met the brothers, he readily recognised that they were hard-working men and with Bruno's support he had no hesitation in backing them. Now down the track, it was obvious that it was the right thing.

He congratulated them and wished them well for the future. He thanked them for the tapestry saying it was something he would always treasure. He added he would remember not to fly too close to the sun (readily grasping the broad hint not to pry or ask too many questions).

Flite though still had a niggle about clandestine activities such as growing of marijuana as a supply source for Bruno. It had never come to light but almost certainly had been going on for a long time.

A couple of weeks later however, one Saturday afternoon unannounced, the sons called at Flite's home. Over a glass or two of wine, they told Flite that the families had got word from their insider police contacts that they had been tipped off about the identity subterfuge. Consequently, they were reopening their investigations into the Garibaldi Club murders with their fathers cited as persons of high interest.

In the light of this, both lots of parents had flown out of Australia to return to the "old country" for an extended stay. The boys said that they would be safe there and would live like royalty. It was unlikely that they could ever return to Australia.

Flite was greatly relieved when they also told him that with the parents gone, they had got rid of their marijuana operation but had kept one or two plants for their own and friends' use. They also divulged that the mystery ingredient in the tomato sauce blending process had been marijuana.

With their supply of this ingredient now gone, the women had decided to include a jug of their home-made grappa in the blending process. Everybody agreed that the new sauce tasted even better.

When leaving, the boys gave Flite a case of tomatoes and a dozen bottles of the new sauce. As they started down the driveway, they called from the car that they had forgotten to mention that they had left a couple of shrubs for Flite down by his glass house.

Finishing off the rest of the wine, Flite reflected on the way the whole venture had successfully and happily turned out. Getting up from his chair, much relieved he commented to himself "I guess it's a case of its all well that ends well!"

But, when he walked down to his glasshouse, he stared in disbelief, standing against the door were three very healthy-looking marijuana plants.

THE COUNCIL DOG-POUND MEN

If you lay blame, ya gotta have the facts

Flite's family had a black and white female Tenterfield Terrier called Snowy. She was a very affectionate, playful little dog without any vicious streak in her bones. She was particularly loved by Flite's young daughters who quarrelled every evening before bedtime as to whose bed Snowy would sleep on that night.

One Saturday morning when Flite was on his motor mower running over his lawn and Snowy was lying on the driveway nearby, the Council Pound truck drew up and two grumpy-looking fellows in uniform got out and walked up to Flite.

Without any how-do-you-do or greeting, the bigger of the two asked Flite very brusquely "Is that your dog?" When Flite replied that it was, the Council bloke thrust a paper in Flite's hand and went on to explain that the Council had received complaints about a little black and white dog menacing and biting people in the area. Two children had needed hospital treatment.

The letter was formal notice that Snowy was to be impounded as a public menace and risk to the community.

Taken aback, Flite asked "Are you sure you have the right dog?"

The Council blokes laughed and said they would not be there if they weren't, adding that the Council had made extensive enquiries and the only small black and white dog in the area was Snowy.

Flite walked over to pick up Snowy saying to the Pound men "You are very wrong!"

The big Council man laughed and sneeringly asked how he could be so sure.

To this, Flite opened Snowy's mouth and said "Have a good look! You can see the dog has no teeth....she just could not bite anyone!"

He went on to explain that Snowy had suffered a severe gum infection some 12 months ago and the vet had removed all her teeth.

The second Council man only uttered "Bloody hell!". The bigger grumpier one grabbed the letter and the pair of them turned, got back into their van, and drove off.

Flite bent down and tickled Snowy's tummy.

"You're not a savage dog are you Snowy?" asked Flite.

As he did so, Snowy just grinned (albeit a toothless grin)

• • • • •

Snowy, a beautiful little dog whom we all loved dearly, died and went to Doggy Heaven on 6th September 2021.

We all miss her.

THAT BAD MAN AGAIN

Apart from being the Group Leader Southern Division, Norman MacLeod had the additional responsibility of supervising the Admin's three messenger staff.

When Tim Flattery started at the NSW Admin., after his initial briefing from the Head Messenger Tommy Perkins he was taken around to meet Norman.

When he knocked on the open door of the office he was brusquely told "come in". He did and stood in front of the desk whilst Norman ignored him and continued writing without looking up. When he did, he squinted at Timothy through his rimless glasses sizing him up. He was aware that Timothy was from Northern Ireland and had served in the British Army.

He wrongly surmised that Timothy because of his Belfast and British army background must be a Protestant Orangeman. He asked Timothy whether he was indeed an Ulster man and Timothy agreed that he was. Then with this seeming corroboration, he asked Timothy in quick succession, did he go to Church, did he read his bible, and did he drink?

Timothy, unaware of Norman's mistaken idea of his religious affiliation, confirmed that yes, he did go to church and that he also read his bible (which was something of a white lie). To the last question, he replied "All Irishmen drink!" Norman turned his nose up at that and went on to stress that Timothy should never drink at work and that any form of dishonesty was regarded seriously and would mean the sack. It was a case of zero tolerance.

Norman dismissed him with the threat that he would be watching his work performance and conduct very closely.

Timothy was not particularly impressed by it all and concluded that he would need to be careful with this podgy little man.

As we already know Timothy, fitted in well and gave no cause for complaint. He presented well, was always cheerful and helpful and very conscientious.

At the end of his six months' probation, Norman had to give him a good performance report which gained him permanent appointment.

He was grudgingly accepted by Norman who called upon Timothy to undertake personal chores for him such as picking up his dry cleaning and even some grocery shopping.

This all changed some months later when Ash Wednesday came along and Timothy with a couple of junior loans officers attended the special Mass at the nearby St. Patricks in Harrington Street at lunch time. They came back with the smudge of ash on their foreheads signifying that they were ash and unto ash they would return.

It was a traditional Catholic thing.

When Timothy came into Norman's office to deliver his inward mail and loan files Norman on seeing the ash mark, hit the roof exclaiming "You are a Catholic?"

He then angrily dressed Timothy down saying you should know that you are not permitted to wear or display anything related to political parties or religious affiliation that might give offence to customers. He ordered him to get the ash off his face immediately. What Norman said, of course, was true but in the Ivory Tower of the NSW Administration Bank customers were rarely wandering the corridors.

After that Norman gave Timothy a hard time taking delight in sending him out in terrible weather or 10 minutes before he was due to knock off to deliver mail to the Head Office Mail Room. He kept him waiting, constantly finding petty fault. Timothy readily recognised what it was all about, he was back again in Belfast. He thought he had escaped all that here in Australia.

Norman regularly criticised him within the senior management group. One morning tea after a tirade from Norman, Flite commented that he was surprised at his criticism as he had always found Timothy excellent and a real staff asset. The other members of the group including Simon Sinclair also expressed surprise. Norman finished his cuppa and left in a huff.

One of the perks of the messenger staff in the autonomous NSW Admin was that two of them were called upon to act as waiters and drink stewards at Bank functions such as luncheons for VIP clients.

They were paid an extra $50 for each function and on the basis that there generally were sometimes two such luncheons a week each of the messengers benefitted with a little bit of extra money. An additional benefit was that after the guests had left and they had cleaned up they had a meal of the leftovers which the catering staff were aware of and made sure there was ample remaining for them.

On this occasion Timothy and the other junior messenger Dutchy (by name Kirt Van Dijk) had looked after the guests, cleaned up and were each getting stuck into some barramundi. There was a bottle of South Australian white wine on the bench with about an inch of wine still in it. Kirt had already had a glass from another almost empty bottle and so Timothy poured it into a glass (there was a mouthful and no more).

Just as he put the glass to his mouth, through the door came Norman McLeod.

Seeing Timothy with the glass at his lips, Norman was livid and went into a frenzy, exclaiming "You know you should not be drinking on duty and furthermore you are not entitled to be drinking the Bank's wine." He was almost frothing at the mouth and his face became as red as beetroot. He called out to the startled Timothy, "You will get the sack for this!"

With that, he scuttled around to Simon Sinclair's office. Simon had his coat off as well as his shoes and tie sitting on his sofa enjoying a quiet whisky and soda when Norman stormed in without knocking. By this stage he was hardly coherent.

Simon could not understand what all the fuss was about so, in the absence of his deputy who was over at Head Office, he buzzed for Flite.

Flite quickly grasped what was wrong. He was fully aware that the practice of the messengers "finishing up" after Bank luncheons had been going on for years and was tolerated by senior management at the highest level. So, in attempting to defuse matters, Flite suggested that before bringing Timothy in that they should talk to Tommy Perkins, the head messenger, about the accepted ground rules and practice.

Tommy was an old Royal Navy Petty Officer who had had two ships sunk under him in World War 2. He was a hard nut and took no nonsense from anyone. When asked about accepted practice Tommy succinctly confirmed (pointedly looking at Norman) that the messengers invariably finished the leftovers including wine. He qualified this by adding no more than one glass was allowable.

If any residue was greater than this, the bottle had to be handed to the Chef for use in her cooking. He confirmed that he had drilled both Kirt and Timothy as to what was right, and he was confident that neither of his boys would breach protocol and suffer the consequences. When Norman angrily proclaimed, "They should not be drinking" Tommy just looked at him and retorted angrily "If they were Mister, they were within their rights!"

Simon was very loath to get offside with Tommy and let it pass.

Kirt was then called. He confirmed that he was aware of what was allowable and what was not and that he had never breached the rules. When queried by Norman, he confirmed he had drunk a glass of wine from an almost empty bottle.

To a further query from Norman, he commented that there was only one other bottle with any wine which had been drunk by Timothy, adding that it would have been lucky to have been any more than a mouthful.

When Timothy fronted, he readily agreed he had drunk a small amount of leftover wine but certainly well short of a full glass.

Before anybody else could say anything, Norman shouted at Timothy, "I warned you about drinking on duty and now you will be sacked!" Turning towards him, Simon said to Norman, "Restrain yourself, you clearly have a set against this man. On the evidence, he has nothing wrong. Technically you are right, but he has followed acceptable longstanding practice. You cannot hang him for that."

With that he told Timothy to return to the reception desk where he was working and that the matter was closed.

Norman was seething with anger and in front of Flite, called Simon gutless and weak for letting the staff get away with inappropriate behaviour. Dismissing Flite, Simon sat Norman down and called for an apology which was grudgingly given. He then told Norman bluntly that he was treading on thin ice, that he did not like the way he had been carrying on about Timothy and that he should pull his horns in.

When asked, Norman said in his view Timothy was lazy and slack and needed to smarten up. (He, of course, never mentioned the real reason.) Simon was aware of Norman's general anti-social attitude and vehement opposition to alcohol. Even before Norman had insulted him in front of Flite, he thoroughly disliked the man but had to tolerate him in the interests of group harmony.

Norman walked away, resolving to get back at Timothy any way he could.

Things seemed to settle down somewhat. Norman never raised Timothy at morning or afternoon tea but watched him like a hawk as to time of arrival and departure, time taken for lunch. Timothy never put a foot wrong.

They never spoke.

Some weeks later, Head Office received a call from Sutherland Hospital Emergency advising that the wife of a staff member working in the CBD had been knocked down on a pedestrian crossing in a hit and run accident and had been critically injured. They recommended that the staff member should get to the hospital as quickly as he could.

The staff member was Timothy Flattery.

It was soon determined that Timothy was with the NSW Admin and the message passed on immediately to Simon Sinclair. He, in turn, buzzed Norman MacLeod and directed him to tell Timothy as quickly as possible and arrange for a bank car to take him to the hospital.

As it happened, Timothy was out of the office on a regular "mail run" around the small ring of CBD branches. He was due back shortly. In the interim, before his return to the office, Norman went into an interview with clients. He left no note for Timothy, nor did he mention the situation to anyone else.

By the time Norman's interview concluded, Timothy had gone to lunch.

Norman went to lunch in the Senior Executive dining room at Head Office at his appointed time and before Timothy had returned. Again, he left no note nor asked anyone to pass on the dire tidings to Timothy.

When Simon Sinclair returned from a visit to North Sydney branch at 2pm there was Timothy sitting up like Jacky at the reception desk. Simon was horrified and exclaimed "What are you doing here still? Don't you know your wife has had an accident and is critical in Sutherland Hospital?"

Timothy blanched and said he had not been told. Simon immediately called his driver who was still in the building car park basement and told him to get Timothy to the hospital as quickly as possible. The driver made good time, but it was too late. When Timothy arrived, Kerry had already passed away. The hospital people and Kerry's parents were understandably angry, asking where have you been? The Bank was told at 11am.

Timothy devastated and in tears could only lamely mumble "I wasn't told!"

The driver took Timothy home and then phoned Simon to tell him of Kerry's death. He was horrified and called Norman in to tell him the news. Norman just shrugged and commented that they had simply missed one another.

Simon was disgusted at his complete absence of any compassion or regret for the failure to pass the message. He expressed his deep disappointment and told Norman, "One way or another I think you are going to regret your behaviour this day!"

A big contingent from the Bank including all NSW senior management except for Norman MacLeod attended Kerry's funeral. It was readily apparent that there was tremendous support and sympathy for Timothy. Referring to the strength of this, Flite commented to his colleagues that it was very fortunate for Norman that his part in Timothy not being present when his wife died was not generally known otherwise, he might well have had a very hard time of it.

To add to Timothy's deep grief, Kerry's autopsy revealed that she was in early pregnancy. She had not mentioned it to Timothy, perhaps because it was early days. The news turned the screw on his heartbreak even more knowing that Kerry and he were both looking forward so much to having children.

The hit and run driver was never found.

Everybody rallied around to offer support. Apart from his fellow staff, his friends in the parish choir were very solicitous, the women bringing him round meals and inviting him home to dinner.

Terry O'Brien told him there was no point in him moping around in his unit by himself with constant reminders of Kerry. The housekeeper's apartment at the rear of the presbytery had been long vacant and Terry said, "Come up here and stay with me boyo in the place at the back!".

He and Terry got on well together. Normally, Terry cooked dinner but sometimes they ate in with takeaway. Occasionally they would have a meal at the pub. Invariably, their Irishness would prevail, and they would down a couple of cans of Guinness or Harp.

On a weekend, after attending to any gardening needs or repairs around the parish enclave, Timothy would jump on his motor bike and go for long rides. When asked he was non-committal but from his few sparse comments, he often frequented the northside parks where he could spend some time in reflection looking through the trees over the harbour waters.

At work, he was quiet but remained conscientious and helpful. The spring though had gone out of his step and on his rounds, he was not his normal cheerful self. On reflection, in the light of subsequent events he was a man haunted, with a mind weighed down by grief. A deep anger burned inside him.

Norman avoided any contact. If he heard Timothy anywhere in the Executive Row, he would hurriedly shut his door or scurry out to the general office. He never criticised Timothy within the senior management group and never gave him any more messenger tasks obviously intended to inconvenience him.

Water flowed under the bridge for a while without any real disturbances within the State Admin.

With the onset of winter, the football season started and staff discussion particularly on a Monday morning after weekend games revolved around the fortunes of their favourite team. There was considerable interest this year in the outcome of the forthcoming Rugby League State of Origin series, a contest of three games held annually mid-week with teams selected from players born in either of New South Wales or Queensland.

A fierce rivalry had developed, and the New South Wales Blues were anxious to overcome a growing dominance by the Queensland Maroons. Staff interest had grown to fever pitch.

As it happened, the Blues lost the first game by one point. In the normal course of things as staff got down to work on the morning afterwards there should have been a constant buzz, talk about the game and where New South Wales had gone wrong.

On this Thursday morning, there wasn't, staff all and sundry being horrified to learn that Norman MacLeod had been shot and killed the evening before as he took out his wheelie garbage bins.

Simon Sinclair, totally disregarded any thought of Norman's wife, bound up totally in what might be the ramifications for himself. It was left to Flite and the state's Deputy State Manager, Les Ferguson to visit her later in the morning to offer their condolences and ascertain whether she needed any assistance.

Her two sons and their wives were already there to console her and keep her company. She was told to contact Les if she required any immediate help.

Simon Sinclair was beside himself, certain in his mind that Timothy was the killer. If he were, there could be unfavourable publicity for the Bank and somehow, this could reflect adversely on his standing. Greatly concerned, he decided that he and Len Ferguson would talk to Timothy and advise him to come clean and go to the police.

When they talked, Timothy was cool, calm, and collected. It was true, he said, that he thoroughly disliked Norman, but he did not "murder" him. He commented "God will see that he gets what he deserves!"

During their enquiries, it was inevitable that the police would call on the Bank to ascertain whether Norman had been involved in any dispute of consequence with clients. Simon mentioned Norman's altercation with

Bruno, but police dismissed him as a suspect immediately. No, they said, it was someone closer.

Simon mentioned the animosity towards Timothy and the detectives immediately pricked up their ears when they learned he came from Belfast and had seen army service in the Falklands.

They told Simon that Norman had been shot from about 100 yards from the park on other side of the street. It had been dark and whilst there was a streetlight, visibility would not have been ideal. The single shot had hit Norman directly in the heart killing him instantly. The accuracy of the shot notwithstanding poor light clearly indicated that it was the work of a trained marksman.

In all the circumstances, Timothy was certainly a person of high interest. When interviewed by detectives, he was unflustered answering questions without hesitation and staring back unwaveringly at his interrogators. He did not noticeably swallow or lick his lips, often perceived as signs of guilt. He repeated what he had told Simon Sinclair "Yes", he certainly did not like Norman MacLeod but "No, he did not "murder" him."

When asked, he told detectives he had spent the evening with Terence O'Brien, his parish priest, watching the State of Origin match on television. This was readily confirmed by Terry who went on to tell the detectives that Timothy was dead against violence following his war experience and the bitterness of his earlier days in Belfast.

When queried, he denied possessing a gun. The church and presbytery were unsuccessfully searched for a weapon.

The investigating detectives had come to a dead end. Everything certainly pointed to Timothy as the likely killer but with the evidence of the priest in his favour and the absence of the weapon he could never be convicted.

Things changed following Norman's funeral. A few evenings later, his next-door family couple were talking about it all when their young son aged 7 piped up to say that he was glad Mr MacLeod was gone as he was a "bad man." On questioning, the parents were horrified to learn that on the couple of occasions Norman had baby-set for them whilst they had gone to dinner, Norman had abused the boy and threatened to kill them if he told.

A search of his study at home, to his wife's utter shame, uncovered a hoard of child pornography. Norman in fact, despite all his claims of being a good Christian was a paedophile, a human being of the worst kind.

For the police, this opened the possibility that Norman had been killed by someone whose child had been abused.

Police followed this line of enquiry for a while but with no leads of any promise they finally abandoned their investigations, and the case went into the archives as another unsolved crime.

Things settled down in the office without any startling happenings.

Timothy continued to perform his duties in his normal conscientious way but was obviously far from being his usual self. Flite, who had taken over the responsibility of supervising the messenger staff, grew concerned.

Things were resolved a few weeks later when Timothy came into his office and resigned. His father had died, and his mother wanted him to return home and takeover running the pub. There was nothing that could be done to change his mind and so after a momentous send off by the NSW staff and another one by Terry O'Brien and members of the choir, Timothy flew off home.

Some six weeks later, Flite received a letter post marked Belfast. When he opened it, the letter explained how Timothy had learned to live again in Australia after the horrors of war. He had loved his job and was fulfilled beyond his dreams when he married his Kerry. This had all crumbled when Norman discovered he was a Catholic and he was confronted with the same bitterness and animosity that he had come to Australia to escape.

The final straw was when he missed being at Kerry's side when she died through Norman's deliberate failure to tell him of her accident.

Weighed down by grief and bitterness, Timothy confessed that he came to perceive Norman as one of the detested Orangemen of his youth.

Whilst in the normal course, his abhorrence of violence should have prevailed but with all that he had been through he lost sight of reality and his mind regressed to the point where he was thinking again like an IRA soldier.

His letter went on to explain how he had reflected on likely behaviour that would provide a suitable opportunity to execute Norman. (In his mind, he had deliberately denied "murdering" Norman because it was not murder as such but an "execution".)

He was at a loss until one evening taking out the parish garbage bins, he realised that this might well provide the opportunity he was looking for.

After determining from the local council that Norman's garbage was collected of a Thursday, he had watched Norman's home on three consecutive Wednesday evenings. He was not disappointed.

When Norman drove home from work on each occasion, immediately after he put his car away, he brought his garbage bins out to the front of his house.

On the day in question, Timothy had left work at his usual time of 5pm and ridden his motor bike directly over to Mosman and set himself up in the park directly opposite Norman's home. Right on cue, Norman had brought out his bins. Whilst it was coming on dark, there was enough visibility from the streetlight. Sighting his target with the help of his telescopic scope, Timothy had a clear shot which unerringly hit Norman's heart, killing him instantly.

Timothy did not need to look closely as he knew Norman would be dead beyond help. With the attachment of the Argie suppressor there was little noise to excite any alarm. Dissembling the rifle and placing it in his saddle bags he had free-wheeled the bike some 200 yards down the street before starting it up and heading for the presbytery at Sutherland.

When he arrived at Tom Ugly's Bridge on the Georges River (the gateway to the Sutherland Shire) he took the rifle parts from his saddle bags and tossed them into the water below.

With the State of Origin match starting on TV shortly there was less traffic on the road than normal. He made good time and sat down in front of the telly with Terry O'Brien some 10 minutes before the match started.

He had not told Terry O'Brien immediately and Terry had been truthful in telling detectives that Timothy had spent the evening with him watching the State of Origin game.

When he told Terry in confession he was horrified. In granting him absolution Terry commented "it was a terrible thing you have done and a serious sin. However, you were provoked beyond belief and no doubt God will understand."

Timothy went on to say that when he got back to Belfast, reality had finally kicked back in and he suffered intense remorse at what he had done. Still grieving for Kerry too, he was seriously depressed.

Awaiting his arrival, his mother had employed her sister's son to run the pub. When Timothy arrived on the scene, he readily perceived that his cousin was doing it well. Realising the man was married with a couple of young kids and had been out of work for a long time, the pub job had come as a godsend. Timothy did not have the heart to put him out of a job. Additionally, he felt washed-out and needed a clean break from things to find himself again. So, to his mother's disappointment, he had walked away.

Timothy said he was not without money and was receiving his British veteran's pension. He was well placed and was confident of getting a job when he needed to. He went on to mention that he had bought a new Ducati touring motor bike and planned to go on a travelling holiday down the famous Wild Atlantic Way, a road that ran down the west coast of Ireland where every day one could see the wild Atlantic rollers coming in.

Timothy concluded by thanking Flite for his support and kindness and asked to be remembered to everybody.

Flite decided it was best to keep Timothy's confidences to himself although with some unexplained foreboding of what the future might hold.

These thoughts were vindicated a fortnight later when he was contacted by a tearful lady, the sister of the barmaid in the Flattery pub.

She told him that Timothy had gone down to a little village in Donegal on a rocky part of the Irish northwest coast and had stayed at the local pub for a few days.

The place, Glencocmille, was famous for its cliffs from which you could readily see the huge Atlantic rollers (often 40/50 feet high) streaming in to crash against the cliffs and sending spray and foam hundreds of feet high.

One morning, he had gone off with some cheese and onion sandwiches and a small bottle of Harp telling people at the pub he was going to walk the Slieve League cliffs which rise high from the ocean. The track he planned to walk namely the "one man walk" is famous throughout Ireland and regarded as one of the most remarkable hikes in the country due to its spectacular views of the coastline. He was warned by the publican that whilst the walk was not normally dangerous you had to be careful and keep a steady head particularly when the district's notorious heavy winds blew in from the Atlantic.

As it happened about midday on the day in question, the morning's overcast, wind free weather rapidly turned savage with gale force winds and heavy rain. The people at the hotel grew concerned. When Timothy had not returned, they went looking for him. They found his haversack (the sandwiches had been eaten, the empty wrappings and empty bottle of Harp inside). His body lay on rocks at the foot of the cliff a bit further on, out of reach of the waves.

It seemed clear his fall was an accident and not a deliberate act.

Where he fell, the path was very narrow and the grizzled old locals at the pub were adamant that he would have been vulnerable with his gammy leg. Probably, they said, blinded by the rain he would have been knocked over by the force of the wind and fallen to his death. It was apparently not the first time, nor would it be the last.

The publican said he had departed in the morning without care. The fact that he had requested the sandwiches and eaten them did not seem consistent with someone intending to end their life.

The local parish priest agreed and gave Timothy a catholic burial with a requiem mass. He was buried in the church graveyard.

She went on to say that all at St. Patricks were devastated and had mourned this poor tragic man. Terry O'Brien had broken down and wept openly at the memorial requiem.

Flite always suspected that without his beloved Kerry, Timothy would lose his will to live. Even so, in view of his catholicity, he doubted his death was suicide. Nevertheless, he wondered, why Timothy purposely put himself in harm's way with his disabled leg to walk this treacherous track. If he did seek death but not by his own hand, was he hoping that the cruel Fates who were always present, might intervene on his behalf. Flite shook his head. Was his death the fulfilment he was hoping for by deliberately placing himself in harm's way or was it really just a terrible accident? We will never know.

Subsequently mourning this poor man's tragic demise, Flite hoped like many others, that Timothy was now in a far happier place in the arms of his beloved Kerry.

HISTORICAL NOTE

An earlier Norman MacLeod

Source: Author unknown and undated
Article: *"Norman MacLeod - The Wicked Man"* - www.wikipedia.org

There was a famous Presbyterian churchman of this name, but he was a far cry from a former Norman MacLeod notoriously known as "the wicked man". This Norman MacLeod was the chief of the MacLeod clan at the time of the Jacobite Rebellion in 1745.

Contrary to many of his kinfolk, he had shrewdly sided with the English Government and did not participate with his clan at the disastrous battle of Culloden. Subsequently, following the victorious Duke of Cumberland's direction to rase the lands of those who had fought with Bonnie Prince Charley's rebels, he and Macdonald of Sleat laid waste to the lands of Grant of Glenmoriston.

They then together attacked the Jacobite MacLeods of Ramsay clan causing considerable havoc, slaughtering many people, killing livestock and destroying houses and boats.

On another occasion, he and the Macdonald again, rounded up the inhabitants of the Isle of Skye and put them on a boat due to sail to the American colony planning to sell all 96 of them there as slaves at three pounds a head. Fortunately, for these people before the boat sailed, it was wrecked in a storm, and they were all able to escape unscathed.

He was also believed to have starved his wife to death by locking her in his castle's dungeon and leaving her there.

Not a nice individual by any account. Almost assuredly, it was his blood that ran in our Norman's veins and not the churchman's.

THE WIFE BETA BETA BRA MEN

Arthur Smythe-Parker was a remittance man. He was the second son of a wealthy, upper class English family. His father was a knight and member of the House of Lords.

He had always been a handful getting into numerous scrapes when he was young. He had been expelled from two elite schools. He was no better in his twenties. Because of his family background, his public drunken antics and brawling regularly featured in the press. He had considerable inherited money but ran up gambling debts which he stubbornly refused to settle. He was pursued but still would not pay and rather than endure the embarrassment of public court proceedings his father settled his debts.

In the end, it was all too much for the family. They bundled him off to Australia with a hefty monthly allowance which they promised to continue provided he gave up gambling and did not get into trouble with the law.

Here, on his own and no longer in the shadow of his titled elder brother, he settled down and generally behaved. He had enough inherited money of his own to buy a unit in the expensive harbour suburb of Point Piper and to drive around in a cream BMW coupe with red leather seats.

He easily gained entry to Sydney A-list society and was warmly welcomed by its matrons on learning his superior upper-crust background. He gained prominence in the social press and was linked there a couple of times with high profile women. However, these romances never lasted.

But he soon tired of it all and decided he needed to get a job.

But what?

When he thought about it, the only thing he really had practical knowledge of was debt collecting from his own experience of being pursued. And so, he thought being on the other side of the fence might be fun and worth a try.

He set up shop at Kings Cross above a strip club and went looking for business from the banks and financial institutions. With his superior attitude, Savile Row suits and gift of the gab in toffee English, he gained access to senior management. He was very convincing.

They tried him out with a few of their worst hard-core cases on the verge of write-off. When he achieved better than fifty per cent in number, he won them over and they started giving him more and more of their delinquent loans to pursue. However, it cost him some thirty thousand dollars to pay out the loans in question, an outlay he considered worthwhile to get himself started. He also recruited to his team a couple of these debtors who impressed with their ability to avoid payment. He and his small team were relentless, aggressive and successful.

Soon, as his reputation spread, it was inevitable that his services would be sought after by the shady part of town, brothel keepers, SP bookmakers, illegal gambling bosses and even drug barons to collect from non-payers. This side of his business had to be handled in a more aggressive manner than recalcitrant bank debtors. Physical persuasion was often required.

To undertake these collections, he employed three young Samoan Island brothers. They were not tall but seemingly as broad as they were tall. They were bearded, dressed in black track suits invariably with their hood up. When Arthur knocked on a front door demanding payment and the debtor looked out to his front gate to see one of these men standing there with a long kendo stick, it was very persuasive.

But they were a handful.

Here, unfettered by their island community constraints, they were running amok, frequently in trouble for drunkenness, brawling and worst of all for abusing their wives. Their girls were sick of the constant trauma and violence. They had gone to Arthur with the ultimatum that if he could not bring about a drastic change and, get each of them a house, they would return home.

If they did, their husbands would be obliged by custom to return with them or be cut off from their family.

Arthur was desperate, he could not afford to lose them.

He did not like his day-to-day contacts at the big banks who full of their own importance talked down to him. In New South Wales, the ABC Bank's hard core debt collection function was part of Flite's responsibilities.

Arthur perceived Flite as a different kettle of fish. He was street wise, approachable and not up himself. They got on well. So, following the wives' visit, Arthur approached Flite seeking his help. Specifically, he asked whether Flite could arrange housing loans for his three employees and their wives provided he guaranteed the arrangement.

They were earning good money and could easily meet any likely loan repayment. Bearing in mind that loans would be restricted to the Bank's normal 80% of security value, this raised the issue of how they were going to meet the residual 20% needed.

Arthur indicated that he would provide any shortfall. He mentioned that notwithstanding their husbands' shenanigans the girls had been controlling the money and had a lot put away. He also agreed to individually guarantee each loan.

Flite agreed in principle to help and visited Arthur's office to talk to the girls. They were delighted with his news, but he cautioned that if any of the men stepped out of line, it was zero tolerance, he would renege on the deal. He was bluffing, of course. He couldn't once it all came to pass but it did put a bit of steel in the girls' determination to make it work.

It all happened. They found apartments in Coogee the girls liked that were within their means and Flite approved the loans.

Arthur read the riot act to his men and frightened them about the consequences if they stepped out of line. There was no way they wanted to return home to the strictures of Island Society.

They quickly recognised that the game was up and that they had to behave or cop community elder censure back home. They gave up drinking and brawling and looked after their wives. They regularly attended a special Pacific Islander church. They saw the light!

Chastened by their own experience, Arthur's men took it upon themselves to counter domestic violence within their community calling themselves the WBBB (Wife-Beta Beta Bra's). They were a formidable trio and, of course, relished the not infrequent physical persuasion required to influence others to forego violence against their women. They earned high praise from their Church's pastor who described them as "The strong arm of God".

Their reputation spread through the Islander and Maori communities mainly through the word of mouth of women and there was strong ongoing demand for their services. They did a lot of good in reducing domestic violence and on a few occasions even persuaded some white mates they played rugby with, to forego abuse and violence.

A television station got to hear of them, and they were featured a couple of times on community programs. Women advocates publicly praised their work.

They also achieved additional fame with their heroics one Saturday morning. They had been painting the inside of one of their homes when they received a phone call from a woman who was a member of their Church congregation. This woman, obviously distressed, hurriedly told them that the woman next door was screaming and obviously being bashed by her partner. She begged them to come quickly to intervene.

When the brothers arrived at the house some ten minutes away, they could hear a woman screaming and calling out "Stop! Please stop!" The front door was closed, and they ran around to the back past an old battered 4-wheel drive with camping gear strapped to the roof. The back door was open and Fetu, the eldest brother, stepped inside.

He immediately saw in front of him this big, bearded man hitting a small woman around the head and shoulders with a doubled up heavy leather belt. She was on the ground, half siting up. Her nose was bleeding and lips cut. One eye was swollen and black.

The man was shouting, "I have had you, you miserable f…king bitch!" As he raised his arm to hit the woman again, Fetu pushed him away, calling, "Stop it, you mongrel!" The man was totally taken by surprise. He had been so engrossed with his attack on the woman that he had not seen Fetu enter through the door.

He glared crazily at him, calling out "Where did you come from you black bastard? Piss off! This is nothing to do with you. Get out of my house or I will give you a bloody hiding too."

Lying unconscious on the ground on the side of the room was a young boy of about twelve or thirteen whom Fetu assumed had tried to defend his mother.

Fetu stood his ground and tried to help the woman to her feet. As he did so, her assailant threw a punch at his head. He ducked and counter punched his opponent violently in the chest. The blow knocked him backwards into a hallway. Getting up, he backed up into the bedroom behind him, emerging a minute later with a heavy rifle.

Pulling the woman to her feet by the hair, he roughly grabbed her by the arm and said, "Get outside and get into the truck." He pushed her towards the door. Fetu, ignoring the rifle, closed with him. The man lifted the butt of the rifle and struck Fetu hard under the jaw. He dropped to the floor badly dazed, all but knocked unconscious.

His brothers standing outside called "Are you OK Fetu?" When there was no reply they started to enter but hastily retreated when a shot was fired towards them.

By this time the police had arrived. It was not the first time, and they knew that this violence was a regular occurrence. The brothers told them Fetu was inside and had tried to intervene. They mentioned the rifle shot.

The police, of course, knew this man well and called to him by his first name to come out of the house with his arms raised. He was cautioned not to do anything silly.

There was no immediate response.

A couple of minutes later, there was a call from inside, "I am coming out with the woman. I am getting into the truck with her and driving away. Don't try to stop me. I will shoot anyone who gets in the way."

With that he grabbed the woman and pushed her in front of him towards the door. The police got behind the truck.

Fetu shook his head and raised himself on his hands and knees. Still groggy, he had heard the big man's threat. He and the woman had opened the wire door to exit the house about 10 feet away. Fetu got to his feet and with a loud, growling roar sprang at the big man's back in a heavy bone-jarring crash tackle. The force of the tackle propelled the man forward causing him to fall heavily on the concrete path. The woman fell some distance in front of him. The rifle was jolted out of his grasp and landed at the feet of the two Samoan brothers.

Two police grabbed him and lifted him to his feet. One held him whilst the young female constable started to handcuff his hands behind his back. They did not frisk him for weapons, the priority being to get the cuffs on. He was aggressive and mouthing profanities. He suddenly head-butted the male constable holding him and broke away from the officer behind him before she got the cuffs on.

He ran at his wife sitting on the low brick fence a few feet away from the younger Bra Boys. Before they could stop him, he had drawn a wicked looking hunting knife from under his jacket and stabbed her three times in the chest.

The boys grabbed and disarmed him. The burly old police sergeant acting summarily, knocked him to the ground. His hands were roughly handcuffed behind his back and he was bundled into the back of the police van.

The woman was lying on her back. She was bleeding freely, and the young police were trying desperately to staunch the flow. She was conscious and told them that her husband had been going away pig shooting with his mates. He had lost his week's pay on the poker machines and had demanded she hand over her credit card so he would have money. When she refused, he went into a rage and started hitting her with the leather belt.

She asked if someone could go and help her son who had tried to defend her. When he had got between them, his father had up-ended the boy, lifted him up and dropped him head-first on to the floor. He had not moved.

When the paramedics arrived they quickly stabilised the woman and stopped her bleeding. They did not think the knife had caused any serious damage. It was different though with her son. He was still unconscious, and the paramedics thought he probably had a fractured skull. The pair were rushed to St. Vincent's Hospital and admitted to the Emergency Ward.

As suspected by the paramedics, the wife recovered without serious injury but carried the scars for the rest of her life. No so her poor young son, he never regained consciousness and died two days later. His neck had been broken and he had a badly fractured skull.

His brutal father, who showed no remorse, was charged with his murder and the attempted murder of his wife. He was made an example of and sentenced to gaol for life. He died there.

His wife who was a registered nurse got on with her life and a couple of years later married a hospital x-ray technician. This was a happy relationship with children, devoid of any of her previous trauma. She often recalled the love of her other son who died in her defence and prayed for his rest.

Fetu was lauded in the media for his heroics and was subsequently formally presented with a bravery award by the State Governor.

It came as no surprise within his community when he was made a Church Elder.

Nobody, of course, ever anticipated the greater good that would flow when Flite agreed to approve those home loans.

Certainly, the Wife Beta Beta Bra wives were very happy at the boys' total turnaround and proud of their anti-violence activities. That was an unexpected bonus.

Arthur also was delighted, as he had his men secure for the long term.

As for the loans themselves, they never missed a beat.

IVAN KATANOV

A KGB Man

The ABC Bank as part of its community relations programme sponsored the annual Greentree Agricultural Field days.

Greentree is a small township in southern New South Wales amid a sound sheep and wheat growing region. The Field Days are a big event on the national agricultural calendar with a hundred or so exhibitors showing and demonstrating their wares from huge tractors and farm equipment to chain saws, freshwater fish fingerlings and sheep dip.

As the major sponsor, the Bank presence consisted of a team of its experts, agronomists, lending people housed in a huge tent from which they dispensed finger food and grog (mostly the latter) to exhibitors for the week of the event.

It was full on! The entertainment never stopped flowing.

One year it was Flite's turn to stay for the duration as the Bank's formal representative. The prime exhibitors that year were Kursk tractors, huge Russian vehicles built like tanks, very robust but with little thought for operator comfort.

With the tractors came a Russian contingent, big rough blokes who could drink like fishes. Not surprisingly, the Bank's hospitality tent ran out of vodka and the team had to go into Greentree for fresh supplies. When these ran out, they had to drive 70 kilometres to the nearest regional centre to collect a truck load.

The tent was continually in an uproar but well behaved. There was no fighting….the Russians being on their best behaviour. Flite was a bit uneasy with it all. However, when Simon Sinclair visited, he saw no problems claiming it to be the best event ever.

Each afternoon at 4pm there was a sky diving event with a team of professionals displaying precise team jumping with delayed opening of chutes, trailing flares etc. It was spectacular.

The Bank's tent was in a clearing between some big gum trees and after watching the show this day there was discussion about how accurate landings could be. One of the Russians (as it turned out Ivan Katanov) was forthright in saying he could jump from 1500 feet guide himself through the trees and land at the front entrance to the tent. He was given a bit of a roasting. So, a bit miffed and probably well primed, he went off to find the plane and pilot. About half an hour later the Cessna buzzed the tent.

The Russians cleared everybody from the front of the tent, and they watched Ivan jump. He was obviously very skilled and easily guided himself through the treetops to land about 10 feet in front of the tent. The mob went wild particularly the Russians vindicated in their national pride.

Flite got to know Ivan well over the next few days. It turned out he was the local manager for an international Russian trading company and had been stationed here in Australia for some four years. He loved Australia and subsequently often said "if I were not a good Russian, I would be an Aussie."

A few days after Flite got back to Sydney, Ivan telephoned him one morning inviting him over to his office for coffee.

At this time, the Russian president Mikhail Gorbachov concerned at the extent of Russian public drinking had issued an edict that their consulates and agencies should go "dry".

When Flite got to Ivan's office, coffee was served in little fine china cups, very dainty and genteel. When this was cleared by his assistant, he locked the door and took a beautiful small timber box off his desk. It had a sliding lid like the pencil cases of old. Inside, very snug, were two shot glasses, and two pewter phials each of which held three shots of vodka! Flite became a little apprehensive when the door was locked. However, Ivan's subsequent comment that "as every Russian who has lived long knows, you must be careful" reassured him somewhat.

And then they were into it. Firstly, they toasted the workers of Australia, then the workers of the Soviet Union, then friendship between their peoples and then the friendship between them.

When the two phials were emptied, Ivan produced a bottle of Russian Thunder vodka from a desk drawer.

After an hour and a half of this rapid-fire drinking, Flite was well on the way to being "legless". He departed as politely and as soon as he could, jumped into a cab to Central Railway and got a train to Liverpool the closest station to where he lived. His wife picked him up and took him home to sleep it off.

He rang the Bank to say that he had come down sick and he was.

Flite made sure he never got into that situation again but over the next couple of years, Ivan and he had occasional lunch or drinks together. Ivan was great company and had a great insight into the wider world.

Ivan's favourite thing was to sit at lunch time in the back bar of the Forbes Hotel in King Street of the city, yarning with a beer and eating meat pies.

His father had been killed in the war and he and his mother had lived with her mother and father in a small apartment in a poor part of Moscow. He had been good at school and gained entry to a Red Air Force academy. He graduated with distinction and after some 5 years in the air force was appointed to Home Security and Internal Affairs. He had spent some time in Great Britain with Aeroflot the Russian national airline and had subsequently come to Australia to manage the Soviet trading agency here.

Whilst he did not talk about it, it was apparent he had good political connections. Flite had invited he and his wife home for a weekend barbecue, but he always declined saying "it would be better if we didn't!"

One afternoon at work, Flite received a hurried call to say that he was returning home urgently. He was flying out that evening to return to Russia and would not be back. He thanked Flite for his friendship and apologized that he had to leave like this.

That was that!

A couple of days later it was revealed that our Ivan was a KGB spy. He had somehow persuaded a prominent Federal parliamentarian to provide insight into the Government's recent weapons purchase from the USA. It was something of a storm in a teacup. There was really nothing significant in what had been passed over and it had already been well canvassed in the freely available military media.

The parliamentary opposition got hold of it and made a fuss to embarrass the Government. To square off, the Government declared Ivan "persona non grata".

Certainly, there was nothing untoward in Flite's dealings with him. He was just a boisterous bloke who came to love meat pies.

Ivan sent Flite a couple of post cards of Moscow and Leningrad as it was then called but nothing beyond that.

Some 18 months later, Flite was at home near Camden one Saturday afternoon when he received a call from "an old friend" who would be passing close by later and asked whether he could call in.

It was a very cold afternoon with a freezing wind from the south. Flite had just come inside from the garden to have a rum and sit by the fire. His wife Judy was away, visiting her brother in Sydney.

About an hour later, a black Mercedes pulled up at the front gate and four big blokes in black hats and long black coats got out. It was like something out of the movies. One of them came in up the front steps. It was Ivan but looking quite different. Now he was sporting a goatee beard and wearing little blue tinted glasses.

Flite said to him "Mate! What are you doing here? They'll hang you if they catch you."

After giving Flite a big bear hug, he explained that he was here on a wheat buying mission after the partial failure of the Russian crop. He had been appointed the head of mission because he knew the Australian way. The beard and glasses were part of his disguise together with another name and passport. It was bloody cold and Flite invited Ivan and his mates inside. They declined but stood in the garage. Flite produced some beer and biscuits and cheese which they wolfed down. The poor bastards were obviously very hungry, so Flite raced upstairs cut some corn beef and pickle sandwiches. They went down like they had not eaten for a week. He then produced an opened three quarters full bottle of Smirnoff which they in turn skalled straight from the bottle.

Ivan related how Flite was a good friend and he apologized about the way he left previously without having the chance to say goodbye properly. His mates had a chuckle when he told them it was Flite who had taught him about meat pies. (He had apparently introduced them to them during their stay in Canberra). Then with bear hugs all-round, they got back into the merc and drove off. Flite never saw him again.

About 12 months later, he received a letter from one of Ivan's sons advising that his Dad had died. The son said his father had got caught up in a leadership conflict among the political hierarchy and had made enemies among the dominant faction. The family had no reason to think he was mentally ill. However, he had been detained in a psychiatric research facility where they suspected he had received involuntary treatment from which he died.

Psychiatric repression was practised in the Soviet Union following Nikita Khrushchev's decision to abolish the notorious gulag prison camp system in 1964 following the death of Stalin. It apparently was still availed of occasionally in the 1980s as a "quiet way" of getting rid of anybody who was gaining too much popular support and becoming a serious threat.

Flite grieved for his friend and regularly toasted his memory with Russian Thunder. He often wondered though about his death and as an active KGB operative what had really been his role here.

THREE UNLUCKY MEN

Bank branches hold lots of money, and it is inevitable that criminal elements, attracted like bees to a honeypot, seek to get their hands on it, one way or another.

It was Mao-tse-tung who famously said that "power comes out of the barrel of a gun" and it is true that the gun is frequently used to forcibly persuade a Bank branch to surrender its cash.

In earlier times, Bank hold-ups were almost endemic in our culture nurtured by Hollywood films which regularly depicted such robberies and the deeds of famous bank bandits such as Jessie James, Butch Cassidy and the Sundance Kid. The popular cowboy films regularly shown at the "Saturday afternoon flicks" years ago invariably included a hold up and a subsequent thrilling chase of the bandits.

In Australia, we have our own long history of bank robbers, led by the legendary Ned Kelly who included bank robberies at Euroa and Jerilderie in his nefarious rampage.

For many years, there was little Banks could do to deter potential robbers. They put tellers into high glass boxes and issued them with revolvers or pistols for protection. God knows though how this would be of much comfort when you looked up to see a man in front of you, pointing a gun and demanding money.

Whilst tellers received regular training and practice, it was inevitable that accidents occurred.

On one occasion at a suburban ABC Bank branch a small group of children from the local primary school had been invited to visit the office.

They viewed the strong room and its door, handled bundles of hundred-dollar notes and counted some coin they were allowed to keep. When the branch opened, they were to have morning tea with the Manager and his wife.

The tellers started bringing out their cash in preparation for start of business. As the last one departed the strong room with his cash tin, the butt of his revolver was hanging out of his trousers' pocket.

Seeing this, one of the young boys asked, "Mister, can we see your gun?" The young teller anxious to oblige put his cash tin down and pulled the gun from his pocket. Somehow, however, it got mixed-up with his key chain and the gun dropped to the floor.

It went off with a loud bang and the slug went through the open strong room door and ricocheted around its thick concrete walls. Fortunately, no one was hit. The kids thought it wonderful and talked about it for weeks afterwards.

Their teachers were horrified and quickly bustled them out of the premises without morning tea, waving aside the Manager's frantic apologies.

The young teller was beside himself sitting in a chair with his head in his hands. The Manager took him into his office and with his Assistant Manager berated him for his carelessness that could have had dire consequences. He was obviously badly rattled and in no fit state to go on to the counter and undertake his telling duties. They called a cab for him and sent him home.

The Manager reported the incident to Head Office. As a result, he was transferred to a "leper colony" within the Bank's Stationery and Machinery Warehouse. There, he and half a dozen similar exiles that the Bank wanted to remove from the normal staff ranks were relegated to storeman duties.

The young fellow had been ambitious and keen to get on. He could see no future as a storeman. Within a couple of months, he resigned from the

Bank to take up a job with a Finance Company. He did well there and progressed rapidly. As it turned out, he was very fortunate.

There were other accidents. Ultimately, the suicide of a young man using his Bank pistol resulted in a total recall of the guns from branches.

Around this time with advances in technology, Banks started to explore new means to deter criminals such as "bandit buttons" that alerted law enforcement services and security video cameras. Their adoption did deter many potential hold-up bandits, but a few still tried their luck.

At one Sydney suburban branch just on closing one Friday, this small, thin man entered the office and busied himself at the writing counter. As the last customer was leaving, he turned with a balaclava over his head and jumped up on the enquiry counter with a sawn-off shot gun. He threatened the staff from doing anything foolish, threw a shopping bag to the teller and told him "to fill it up". The teller cleaned out his note drawer and threw the contents into the bag (including a dye bomb device which would spray an indelible dye over anybody attempting to open-up what appeared to be a genuine note bundle).

The bandit jumped off the counter and ran out the front door pushing past the junior clerk doing "closing duty" there, unaware of what had just happened inside.

To minimise loss from hold-ups, tellers were instructed to retain only immediate needs in their cash drawers. Whilst this was impractical at busy times when a lot of cash was being deposited, tellers were well drilled.

Fortunately for the Bank, the teller at the branch had complied and only minutes beforehand had placed five thousand dollars in $50 denomination into the emergency cash safe at his feet.

The thief thus only netted a somewhat meagre five thousand dollars albeit with very little effort.

This was only one of a spate of hold-ups of Sydney suburban banks at that time where the bandits had stood up on the counter threatening customers and staff. There were also a couple of instances where they had climbed over the counter into the staff area.

In the light of this, Insurers recommended to Banks that they should explore the possibility of installing bandit resistant barriers to block access.

One type of barrier adopted, consisted of bullet-proof laminated glass or plastic, extending the length of the counter and rising almost to the ceiling. In front of the teller, just above the counter, there was a narrow slot under which deposits and withdrawals were passed. Above this, at face level, there was a round hole through which teller and customer could converse.

This barrier admirably achieved its purpose but fell out of favour a little because, particularly with heavy external traffic noise, conversations were sometimes inaudible.

The other type of barrier consisted of a steel screen installed in the counter itself. When activated at the push of a button, the screen would rise extremely quickly to the ceiling. It was very sensitive, and staff had to warn customers about it. In the early stages following installation until technicians finally fine-tuned it, it would suddenly fly-up without warning, scaring the wits out of customers and staff.

Again, this device was effective in that it safely secured staff from any threat and prevented access. It was decided to install this type of barrier at the branch recently held up.

Not long afterwards, lo and behold, the small, thin man turned up immediately after lunch, on a day when there was little customer activity. Wearing his balaclava, he jumped up on the counter and demanded staff and the three customers lie on the ground. Then throwing a shopping bag to the teller, he said, "OK son, I am withdrawing again. Fill it up but leave out that dye thing this time."

The teller hit the barrier button. The steel screen erupted from its bed in the counter. The heavy screen rising at great speed caught the bandit between the legs and lifting him up, holus bolus, pinned him to the ceiling. He was screaming in pain. He dropped his sawn-off shotgun on the staff side of the counter. When staff released the barrier, he fell in front of them writhing in pain. The customers had disappeared.

The police arrived minutes later and arrested him. He was obviously badly hurt and was taken to hospital by ambulance under police guard. There he was quickly examined and then urgently operated upon. He was a mess : his pubic bone had been fractured, his genitals crushed, and he was bleeding internally. The doctors were good and did their best for him. In time, he recovered but he had completely lost the wherewithal to father children.

He subsequently confessed to several other bank robberies. When the case went to court, he was convicted and sentenced to seven years gaol.

It is oft said "that crime does not pay" and it certainly was the case in this instance. He subsequently had ample time on his hands to reflect on his misdeeds and their consequences.

It is worthwhile mentioning that when he arrived home from the first robbery, he left the loot on his kitchen table. His mate who drove his get-away car opened the bag and unknowingly, took out the dye bomb device disguised as a bundle of $20 notes. It exploded covering him, and all around him in indelible purple dye.

It was a month before he could get it off sufficiently to leave the house.

GEORGI PAPAS

His Odyssey

Georgi Papas was born at Lyon in France of Greek parents who had left their mythical island of Ithaka, home of the legendary Ulysses, the Hero of Troy, for a better life working in the fine restaurants for which the city was famous.

For all its fame and popular tourism, jobs on Ithaka were scarce and tightly held within families. Unless you were of blood, it was virtually impossible to break in and consequently, it was commonplace for Ithakians to leave the island to seek a better living elsewhere. In the Papas family's case, they gravitated towards gambling casinos or restaurants where existing family contacts ensured their employment.

Georgi's parents Mimi and Nic, had been eking out a meagre existence on Ithaka, selling Nic's daily fishing catch on the wharf of Vathi Harbour. They realised that unless they went where prospects were better, they would always be poor.

So, following the steps of other family members, they had moved to Lyon and readily found work through family contacts at the lower end of the restaurant trade, washing dishes, clearing tables and eventually waiting on customers and assisting as kitchen hands.

Life was certainly better, but they realised they would never be rich until they had their own business.

One uncle, Paulos, had emigrated to Australia some years earlier and had done well for himself as a wholesale fish merchant in Sydney. On his recommendation of better prospects, the family Mimi and Nic, Georgi and his two older sisters emigrated. Paulos set them up in one of his apartments and immediately put them to work in his retail outlet at the Sydney Fish Markets.

Paulos was a wealthy man. In addition to his retail and wholesale businesses he also owned a fishing trawler as well as a popular seafood restaurant in the up-market suburb of Double Bay.

He had never married and was delighted when family members joined him in Australia. He had a reputation as a hard man, a brawler and someone not to trifle with. But he never displayed this side of himself with the family.

One Sunday evening, after the whole family group had enjoyed dinner together Paulos started showing Georgi, who was then aged 10, the rudiments of poker. Georgi was a quick learner and from then on, he always carried a pack of cards in his pocket, continually shuffling them and dealing hands in make believe games. He also got to learn sleigh-of-hand "magical" tricks. At 15, he was almost a professional, always ending up a clear winner in the family's regular poker games.

Nic and Mimi were anxious to get into their own business. Whilst all the family worked hard both at the Fish Markets and at the Double Bay restaurant, they had not accumulated a lot of money. They needed to pick their mark wisely, preferably a place attracting people where they could achieve big volume with good down-to-earth food. And so, when a shop with an upstairs living area came up for lease in Darlinghurst a residential suburb just out of the city in a popular small restaurant strip, Nic grabbed it. Paulos encouraged them all the way.

Nic's Hamburgers place became an instant hit with Sydneysiders. As you drove up Oxford street from the city, there was this big red neon sign, "Nic's Hamburgers" and an outline of a red devil with pitchfork and all.

Not only hamburgers but the grilled fish, souvlaki kebabs and his wonderful Greek salad and baklava cakes drew a constant stream of customers. They opened from 7am to 10pm. Nic and Mimi started to save. In a couple of years, they were able to purchase the freehold of their shop and apartment. Life was good.

Georgi had breezed through school but except for the cards, he had no interest in any other life path. They were his obsession. As soon as he finished work around 7pm, he would shower, put on his suit and catch a cab outside the shop to one of the illegal casinos not far away in Surry Hills.

Whilst he was good with the cards, he was up against cheating professionals. In their customary way, they let him win a bit then started to fleece him. He could not understand what was happening. On the few occasions when his uncle Paulos sat in with him, he won. The rogues were too frightened to try anything with a known formidable character like him.

But over the next six months he lost $20,000 that he could not pay.

His ABC Bank branch manager let him overdraw on the strength of his family connection to the extent of $3,000 but no more. He started issuing cheques for his gambling debts which were dishonoured. His creditors started chasing him with dire threats. He sought safety working on his uncle's trawler to escape them.

Not wishing to worry his parents, he confided in Paulos. Paulos was understanding but made no offer to help him financially. What he did suggest, however, was that he get out of Sydney for a while, go visit the old family in Ithaka until the heat here dies down. Paulos bought him a return airfare to Athens, gave him $3,000 spending money and said, "Get out of here, before you end up at the bottom of the harbour!"

His parents gave him their blessing with Mimi, thinking ahead, that he would inevitably bring home an Ithakian bride.

And so, he left, just a few steps head of the posse chasing him.

Georgi had never been to Greece. Athens was a real eye-opener for him as he visited the famous sites like the Acropolis and the many museums.

He became infused with pride in his heritage. This was further reinforced when he arrived in Ithaka and the family told him the story of the island's legendary Ulysses, his plot of the Wooden Horse that led to the fall of Troy and his subsequent 10 years odyssey voyage after the Greek victory.

Georgi thought how wonderful it was that he carried the blood, admittedly many times removed, of people who must have shared the life of this legendary hero.

He lived with the family sharing their lives working on the fishing boats and celebrating the many religious feast days. It was a good but simple life and he really enjoyed it.

The women in the family did not need any prompting from Mimi and did their utmost to get him married off. He politely declined their solicitations declaring he was not ready just yet.

He was not without money. He still had most of Paulos' money as well as the funds Nic was remitting to him weekly. He was able to be generous to the family and they loved him.

The old men were inveterate card players and a couple had been croupiers at the Monte Carlo Casino. They honed his card playing skills and taught him the signs to look for when he was being cheated. They also taught him card numbering tricks for black-jack and the ploys employed by casino house bankers in baccarat to give them a winning edge. They cautioned him about roulette saying whilst it was illegal, most casinos took measures to protect themselves against large losses.

But after some eight months, he began to get itchy feet and started thinking of where he might go next. He remembered his early life in Lyon and thought it might be good to return and see the place again. The fact that there were casinos there where he could try his luck was an added attraction.

With a letter of introduction from the family, he flew from Athens to Lyon. The family contact was the Maitre de Maison at the Chez Jean-

Paul Huitres et Coquillages restaurant famous for its oysters. With his letter, he was immediately put on as a waiter. With his good youthful looks, baby-speak French and sea food knowledge gleaned from working for his uncle, the customers, particularly the older women loved him and were generous with their tips.

His skill in shucking shell oysters at the table and talking about the different types and sauces impressed the clientle. Jean Paul, the restaurant owner, readily agreed he was a worthy acquisition to his team.

He reinforced this a few weeks later at the end of March when he explained that it would soon be April 14th the seventieth anniversary of the sinking of the Titanic. He explained that on that fateful evening on the first-class dinner menu there was an entrée, Oysters a la Russe (i.e. Russian style). The Titanic version was rather complex and in lieu, he suggested they serve the oysters lying in the half shell in a bed of vodka, sprinkled with black caviar and a dash of Tabasco.

Jean Paul, the Patron, Spiro the Maitre de and the Head Chef sat down together each with a dozen oysters prepared this simple way with a cold, crisp, dry white Picoul de Pinet from the south. They were ecstatic and congratulated Georgi for his innovative suggestion.

The restaurant made a big thing of it, featuring parts of the Titanic menu and highlighting Georgi's version of Oysters a la Russe. The night was a huge success and Oyster a la Russe Georgi style became a permanent feature of the menu.

But constantly coming up in Georgi's mind was the desire to try his hand at the local gambling tables.

So, after finishing work each evening about 10.30pm, he started hot footing it to the nearest of the city's casinos in the next block. However, he did not rush things. Quite apart from anything else, he had little cash to play with.

When he arrived in Lyon, he had some 45,000 francs in his Banque Nationale de Paris account (at the then exchange rate of 8.5 francs to the U.S. dollar – a bit more than U.S.$5,000). His living expenses were minimal, and he was able to bank most of his weekly wages and tips.

So, for the next week, he simply wandered around observing the different gaming venues. He took particular interest in the blackjack tables, just watching and playing over in his mind how he would play the cards dealt to individual players and practising his card count as the old uncles had taught him.

When he started to play, he played cautiously not betting a lot. But he won. As his confidence increased, he raised his stake. He still won. Within the month, his "bank" had increased to 450,000 francs (roughly U.S.$50,000).

It was inevitable that he would come under surveillance by the Casino security people. However, he had learned his lessons on how to hide his card counting. Knowing he was being watched, he moved to the baccarat tables. Here he watched trends of the winning streaks by either the player or the croupier (banker) and when he gauged who was on a roll, he bet on them. He invariably won on the night but to a lesser extent than on blackjack.

His "bank" now stood at 530,000 francs (U.S.$62,000 at the then rate). He was not happy playing baccarat and wanting a break from blackjack, he thought he would have a go at roulette notwithstanding the old uncles' warning.

The roulette table fascinated Georgi, the way the croupier spun the wheel, threw the little white ball in the opposite direction and watched it run, seemingly with a mind of its own. Sometimes it would quickly fall into a slot. At other times, it would roll on and on before doing so.

He spent every evening for a week just watching. Yes, it was possible to win big if you were lucky enough to select a number where the little white ball fell but with 35 possibilities the odds were certainly against you.

Your best chance was the even money bet, black or red but if you won, you only won your stake. You could bet on a cluster with better odds (17½ to 1). He noticed, however, that when big money was bet on a cluster and the house stood to lose heavily, the little white ball finally fell into the cluster on the other side of the wheel.

He continued to watch betting occasionally 2,000 francs on red or black. He certainly was not getting rich this way.

On table 3 that Georgi favoured, there was a maximum payout limit of 1,000,000 francs (about U.S.$120,000 at the then rate) to protect the casino against excessive losses. In practice, bearing in mind the 35:1 payout in the event of a winning number, it was impractical to bet any more than 28,500 francs (28,500 x 35 = 997,500).

It was, of course, possible for more than one person to bet on a specific number and the total combined stake to be greater than 28,500 francs. In that event, if that number won, the casino would be obliged to pay out a greater sum than 1,000,000 francs. But interestingly, Georgi noted, again, such numbers never won.

Was the croupier able to manipulate the result? It seemed a possibility.

He went up to the mezzanine lounge overlooking the tables and started to note the winning numbers when bets on a single number exceeded 28,500 francs. It did not happen a lot but invariably occurred when a group of high rollers visited the table. People generally have their own "lucky number". For example, "8" is considered lucky by Chinese gamblers, others like "7" or "13". However, as most croupiers will tell you, the most common choice of players is "17" which is in the centre of the wheel and is embedded in roulette folklore as the number which has delivered legendary wins.

It did not strike him at first but over time as he kept watching over several nights he noticed that the same set of numbers kept recurring in sequence. Specifically, if number 7 were the first winning number when the house stood to incur a big loss, the same sequence of numbers to evade big payout followed in turn…… 3, 15, 2, 6, 11, 10, 33, 31, and 29. When he studied the numbers on the (European) wheel, it all fell into place. Starting at number 7, the following numbers in his recorded sequence were each separated by three other numbers. Numbers 29 and 7, however, were adjacent to one another. When 29 won, the next number to avoid a big loss was number 7 alongside it, and the sequence started all over again. This pattern was repeated three times whilst he watched.

Somehow, whenever a potentially large win was possible the croupier was able to direct the little white ball to the next number in the sequence and ensure there was no big win payout.

This was, of course, illegal then and still is. However, human nature being what it is, the old American adage of "never give a sucker an even break" still holds true in gambling culture world-wide.

It was true for Georgi too. The next time after one of these numbers won and there was big money on the table, he put 10,000 francs on the next number in his sequence. He won 350,000 francs and went home. He had "cracked" the system.

He waited until the following Saturday evening to visit the casino.

He arrived about 11pm to find the place crowded and buzzing. Elegant European women with fat old men mingled with loud, rude Americans, inscrutable Asians, black bearded middle eastern men and dark Africans.

They all oozed money and happily from the casino's view point all anxious to win more. Big money was being bet everywhere.

On table 3, Georgi watched as three Arab men each placed 30,000-franc chips on three separate numbers. If any of these numbers on which 90,000 francs had been bet had won, the house would have been confronted with a payout of over three million francs.

A potential big hit for sure but not unexpectedly as far as Georgi was concerned, number 6, a number on his list won.

The Arabs bet again as before. Heeding the uncles' advice not to draw attention to himself, Georgi bet 15,000 francs on number 10, the next number on his list. He won 525,000 francs. His bank now stood at 1,400,000 francs. (about U.S.$165,000). He was elated and went up to the lounge and thought about what he should do next.

Looking down to the tables, he saw that a fresh group of croupiers had come on duty at midnight. The new croupier on table 3 would be unaware of his earlier win. He rejoined the crowd around table 3. When big money was bet, one of his numbers won.

More big money was put on the table and plucking up his courage he bet 25,000 francs on his next number. He won 875,000 francs.

He cashed in his chips and deposited his winnings to his bank account at the 24/7 Banque Nationale de Paris banking kiosk adjacent to the casino cashier counter. His bank account now stood at 2,280,000 francs (about U.S.$270,000 at the then rate).

When he returned the next evening, he was confronted in the foyer by two security men who barred him from entry and escorted him to the security manager's office. This official brusquely told him he had been under surveillance. Whilst they were unaware of how he had done it, it was obvious he had gained insight into the casino's system and as such, he was no longer welcome on its premises. He protested his innocence but the security manager in typical Gallic style just shrugged his shoulders and picking up a cigarette, waved him away.

He spent the next few days saying goodbye to friends he had made particularly the people at the Chez Jean-Paul Huitres et Coquillages. Jean-Paul, Spiro and the rest of the team gave him a rousing send-off when the restaurant closed the night before he was to leave.

The next day with a big hang-over he flew back to Athens and caught the ferry to Ithaka.

The family made him very welcome, particularly when he handed them a gift of U.S. $5,000.

Georgi was grieved to learn that his old uncle mentors had died in the interim. He visited their graves and drank a couple of ouzos there whilst he thanked them for their help. He poured the remains of the bottle on their graves knowing they would like that.

The old aunts perceived him now as possessing even greater potential as a husband and pushed several beautiful young cousins at him. But no, he was not yet ready for marriage.

He was getting homesick and after a few weeks he crossed over the water to Athens and caught the plane back to Sydney.

The whole family was there to meet him, Nic and Mimi, his two sisters and uncle Paulos. Mimi and the girls gushed over him excitedly and he warmly embraced his father and uncle.

Things had changed somewhat since he had left Sydney. Nic had fallen at Darlinghurst a couple of times and subsequently had difficulty getting to and from their first-floor apartment and the restaurant. He and Mimi ended up selling Nic's Hamburgers and bought a nice older home at Kingsford near St. Spyridon's Greek Orthodox church.

The two girls had married Australian-born Greek boys and Nic and Mimi had bought each of them a terrace home in nearby Paddington.

Paulos, to preserve family honour, had paid Georgi's gambling debts.

At the big family dinner that evening Georgi recounted the story, of his stay with the family in Ithaka and of his return to Lyon and of working at the Chez Jean-Paul Huitres et Coquillages. He then took them all by surprise by telling of his gambling wins and handing his parents a cheque for $10,000 and each of the girls $5,000.

He warmly thanked Paulos for his support, handing him a cheque for $25,000 which, of course, included payment for settling his gambling debts.

The question then arose of what he was going to do now, now that he was back. His parents no longer had Nic's Hamburgers. Georgi laughed and said, "We will start it up again but a bit differently."

His idea was that the family should go into the restaurant business again but in a more formal, up-market way. He had nearly $350,000 (in Australian currency) to invest and he would borrow what else he needed.

He and Nic would look after the cooking side of things, Mimi would look after the front of the house and the girls and other cousins would attend to the tables. There was stunned silence for a moment then they all erupted in exuberant approval, clapping their hands and thumping him on the back enthusiastically.

The next morning, Georgi and his parents sat down together and drew up a plan.

The first thing was to find a suitable property to lease. Within a week, Paulos had found a place on the main Anzac Parade between the Kensington and Kingsford shopping strips. It was a double fronted shop with lane down one side with good parking space behind it. The old Greek man who owned it though did not want to lease. He wanted a buyer.

Nic and Mimi had already bought the daughters a home. Previously it had always been understood that when Nic and Mimi retired the Nic's Hamburger business would become Georgi's. But it had been sold.

Having bought the two terraces, Nic was strapped for cash. Georgi couldn't so Paulos stepped in and bought it and leased it to Georgi but at the going commercial rate. For Paulos, business was business.

The family got to, to fix the place up. Nic got all the kitchen equipment he needed second hand. Georgi and the girls painted the place from top to bottom. However, Georgi had grand ideas for furnishing the place based on his experience at Lyon and it all cost money.

The floor tiles and columns in foyer resembled marble. They weren't but still cost a packet. The chairs he chose were very ornate with blue silk cushioning. The plates, glassware, cutlery and napery were all top quality. There were murals painted on the walls of the Acropolis and galleys on the ocean.

Statues and busts of ancient Greek notables, Pericles, Socrates, Aristotle and of course, Ulysses were scattered around the room.

This ate up money. He still needed to install air conditioning, fire alarm and sprinkler system, security alarms and acquire a stock of worthwhile wine and liquors. Toting things up, he estimated he needed another $250,000.

He went to his ABC Bank branch in Oxford Street but without security they could not help.

He approached his parents as to whether they might guarantee him and put their home up as security. Bearing in mind that their business that was to go to Georgi had been sold, they readily agreed.

The Bank people took pains to explain to Nic and Mimi that if Georgi defaulted, they would be called on to take over repayments. They were also appropriately cautioned that if no repayments were forthcoming the Bank could move to sell the house to obtain repayment. Nic brushed matters aside, commenting, "It will never happen."

Georgi got his loan and finished off the restaurant to his satisfaction. It was, in fact, they all agreed a veritable show place. Mimi and Nic were very proud of Georgi's vision and its outcome.

At the Sunday night family dinner before the grand opening, Paulos asked whether they had a wine waiter. When they looked at him blankly, he told them he had just the man for them, a Greek Cypriot who had spent a lot of time in Africa.

The next day he brought Demetios in to meet them. He was not a big man but whip tough. His face was very tanned and obviously he had been exposed to a lot of sun. His head was closely shaven, and he sported the biggest walrus moustache waxed to a point at each end. He held himself very erect and cut quite an imposing, authoritative figure. He was very quietly spoken and did not say much when he inspected Georgi's wine stocks. His only comment was "They will do!"

The Ithaka opened in a fanfare of publicity. At the grand opening, the premises were blessed by the Greek Archbishop for Australia.

A swag of notables from the Greek community and a coterie of high-flying individuals, politicians and captains of industry were also there to demonstrate their support.

Simon Sinclair was there (he would never miss a freebie) and basked in the adulation when Georgi acknowledged the Bank's help.

Not surprisingly, the restaurant was a roaring success from the first day it opened its doors. The public flocked in to enjoy Nic's cooking. The old staples from Nic's Hamburgers were there plus a few of Georgi's special recipes that he had picked up overseas including his Oysters a la Russe.

The newspaper critics were ecstatic, and this added further to the restaurant's popularity. Soon you had to book a couple of weeks ahead to secure a table.

Demetios quickly became an icon with his magnificent moustache, authoritative attitude and short gruff comments. The patrons loved him, and he was frequently called upon to pose for photographs with diners.

He turned out to be a surprise packet in other ways.

One Friday afternoon when the staff were cleaning up after lunch and setting up for dinner, a tall black youth entered through the half-closed doors and producing a knife, confronted Mimi at the cash register demanding money.

Demetios was about ten feet away with his back to the foyer. When he heard Mimi's, half stifled scream he turned and grasped the situation in a flash. He quickly strode into the foyer and shouted in a strange language at the youth.

As he drew close, the youth menaced him with the knife and Demetios responded in the same language. Then, it all happened very quickly. Demetios grabbed the youth's wrist and brought his arm down hard on the reception counter causing the knife to fall to the floor. In a quick movement, Demetios drew a wicked looking curved knife from somewhere and held it at his throat. The youth lost his bravado.

Demetios snarled at the youth who replied in timid fashion. After a couple of responses, Demetios seemed to soften and turning to Nic and Georgi standing anxiously behind him, said "It is OK! He is really alright. The poor bastard hasn't eaten in three days."

He then said to Nic and Georgi put some food for him in take-away containers in a shopping bag. When this was done (and still holding his knife at the youth's throat) he said to Mimi "Give him 70 dollars."

With that, he spoke harshly to the youth waving his knife in his face. Then taking him by his right wrist, he held it on the reception counter and made a shallow cut right across the back of the hand where it joined the wrist. The youth was now obviously terrified beyond belief as Demetios pushed him out the door with his shopping bag and the $70.

They all looked at him in amazement and Georgi said "Demetios, I think you need to explain yourself to us particularly how you knew how to talk to him."

Demetios sighed and said "ïts a long story."

When they had sat down at a nearby table Demetios began. "I grew up on my parent's vineyard at the north-eastern end of Cyprus, not far from the

Turkish enclave. When I was 18, my parents were murdered by Turkish gunmen in the intermittent fighting between our two communities.

I had nothing in Cyprus, no uncles, aunts or grandparents, all dead or emigrated. So, I took a ship to Marseille and joined the French Foreign Legion.

I served with the Legion for some 30 years fighting in all their wars in places such as Chad, Dahomey and Algeria in North Africa. I was offered officer rank but declined to leave my friends. I ended my career as the equivalent of Sergeant-Major (Adjutant-chef). (The fierce moustache went with the rank!)

After discharge from the Legion, I fought as a mercenary for several individual warlords, each striving to gain power in different newly emerging countries such as the Congo. But it was very brutal, and I got sick of it. When my two mates got killed in a skirmish, I deserted, got a berth on a Greek tanker heading for Australia, a place as far away as possible from Africa. Not knowing anybody here, I went to the Greek Church people for help. They put me in touch with Paulos who gave me a job on his trawler.

When he found out I knew about wine, I have been helping out at his restaurant as a wine-waiter."

Explaining further, "the Legion", he said, "consists of men from many countries. My two closest friends were Sudanese, good tough soldiers and very loyal friends. When we were in the ranks, of course, we spoke Legion-French but together we spoke Sudanese Arabic. I just picked it up over time associating with them.

Both came from Southern Sudan where face scarring is practised by both men and women. It is an honoured initiation thing identifying you as a member of a particular tribe. When I saw that young fellow, he was tall, black and had the three parallel lines on his forehead denoting he was a member of the Dinkas, like my two friends. I thus knew where he was from and the language he spoke."

When I first called out to him "Hey you Forgotten of Allah pariah dog, what do think you are doing?" It really shocked him saying "Roumi (infidel) how is it that you speak as a follower of the Prophet?"

In talking, it came out that he had come to Sydney to take up a job in the Botanical Gardens after completing his apprenticeship in horticulture at the Newcastle Gardens where his father also worked. Unfortunately, he had come down a week early and was not due to start until next week. He had paid his boarding house landlord for the next four weeks but had his wallet stolen the first night at his lodgings.

The boarding house did not provide meals and he had been wandering around aimlessly trying to cadge food but with little success. He had passed the Ithaka desperately hungry, smelled food and seeing the door open, came in to hold us up on the spur of the moment.

I didn't think he was a bad kid when I heard his story and I thought we should help him."

"Fair enough" said Georgi. "But what was the cut on the wrist all about?"

Demetios laughed and explained, "In the Q'ran, the penalty for theft is loss of the right hand. I told him that unless he repaid the cash, we gave him, it was theft and as such I would find him and cut it off! The $70 would give him $10 a day until he received his first pay. I am certain, he will be back."

And he was, some two weeks later, the youth returned and very deferentially handed Demetios the $70.

Georgi asked about the very nasty looking knife that Demetios had produced. Demetios let them look at it, commenting that he had taken it off a murderous blue-veiled Taureg raider who had tried to kill him with it. He did not elaborate and none of his listeners were game to ask.
This episode cemented the family's relationship with Demetios. When Mimi learned he was sleeping in a shed at the back of the wharf where the trawler was berthed, she offered him the granny flat at the back of their home in Kensington.

Demetios accepted very gratefully and with tears in his eyes, murmured his thanks saying this was the first decent private living quarters he had had since his parents were killed. He was now part of the family.

He declined invitations to come eat with them during the week but always accepted the invitation for the big family dinner on Sunday evening. On these occasions, he would never say much but just sit in a corner sipping his ouzo and watching the daughters' kids play.

Georgi eventually got sick of his mother's nagging and returned to Ithaka to marry a local girl his aunties selected for him. When they returned to Sydney, they married again at the family's St. Spyridon Church at Kingsford.

What an event that was .... a cavalcade of white limousines, the bride arriving in a carriage drawn by two beautiful white horses, trumpets, white doves and 150 guests including the bride's mother and father, brothers and sisters and a dozen of the aunties and uncles from Ithaka.

The wedding reception at a top restaurant on the harbour foreshores was magnificent. Paulos, who was Georgi's best man, not wishing to be outdone in the eyes of the many Greek guests supplied lobster for everybody.

Demetios was the proud groomsman, and it was he who initiated the Sirtaki, the traditional Greek bride's line dance where everybody joins in.

The couple honey-mooned on the beautiful Sunshine Coast of Queensland and returned to Georgi's unit overlooking Bronte Beach. He and Maria were very happy and within 18 months they were the parents of a bouncing baby boy, spoiled rotten by doting grandparents, Nic and Mimi.

The restaurant continued to prosper. However, age was catching up on Nic and Mimi and they decided to retire. A young hard-working couple from the Ithaka family came out to fill the gap and quickly fitted in.

One afternoon getting close to 3pm the lunch people had all left except for a bearded, well-dressed man drinking coffee. He called a waitress over and asked her could she ask Georgi to come out and see him.

When Georgi came out, the man invited him to sit down, saying "I have a proposition for you." He continued, complimenting Georgi on the restaurant and then asked him "What kind of fire protection have you got?" Georgi pointed to the sprinkler system in the ceiling and mentioned his insurance company. The bearded man laughed and said, "No, what I meant is what protection have you got against somebody who doesn't like your food, burning the place down?"

Georgi looked at the man half-puzzled. The bearded man spoke again, "Georgi, for the small sum of $5,000 a month I can guarantee that that won't happen."

Georgi got to his feet angrily and told the man to get out. He did but when paying his bill, he called back to Georgi, "Think about it. I will call you next week for your answer!"

At the subsequent conference, Paulos and the family unanimously agreed not to pay. Demetios, however, said "Pay him a couple of times to give me time to find out where he lives so I can kill him." The family protested that he could not do that, but Demetios just shrugged. When the bearded man rang back, Georgi told him they wern't coming to the party and the caller hung up. Georgi arranged for his security firm to make more frequent inspections of the premises during the night.

Demetios offered to sleep there but the family would not hear of it.

A week went by, two weeks, a month, two months … nothing. Was it all a bluff?

It wasn't. One Sunday morning about 3am, Georgi was contacted by his security firm to say his restaurant was ablaze with the fire brigade making every effort to quell the fire. When Georgi, Nic, Paulos and Demetios arrived, all they found was a smoking, smouldering ruin. There was nothing that could be salvaged.

Paulos was beside himself. His building had gone.

Georgi cried bitterly. The others tried to console him saying "We will build it again!"

Demetios was ominously silent.

When they approached their insurance company, it declined to pay up suggesting that the arson might well have been perpetrated by the family themselves. They needed to investigate.

Paulos, exceedingly incensed, persuaded the Greek Orthodox Archbishop for Australia to make personal representations on the family's behalf and to vouch for them. At Paulos' insistence, there was also a thinly veiled threat in honeyed priestly words that continuing refusal to pay up might well alienate the strong local Greek community.

The insurance company caved in and paid.

The family moved quickly to rebuild and start again but it would be more than 12 months before the premises could be rebuilt and re-furbished again.

The Bank, however, was not happy with the delay. With no revenue from the restaurant Georgi could not make repayments on his loan nor could his parents. He applied for hardship consideration. Whilst Simon Sinclair was sympathetic to the request for alleviation, the Deputy Managing Director, a friend of the deceased Norman MacLeod and similarly bloody-minded was not. Notwithstanding that they were well secured, he gave them three months interest only, principal free deferment. He was adamant that if by then normal repayments had not resumed, the Bank would look to realise on the property. (The property then, in the mid-1980s was valued at $700,000. Georgi's debt $238,000. Today, it is worth more than $2 million).

When Simon Sinclair sought to have the decision reviewed he was firmly told to get on with it. When he told Georgi and his parents they were horrified. Where would they go? Georgi was devastated and ashamed that he had brought this grief to his parents.

Yes, the Bank had told them this was possible, but they had dismissed the notion, thinking it would never happen. They initially tried to keep the news away from Paulos but Mimi, broke down in tears one Sunday afternoon and poured out everything to him.

Paulos, once again the White Knight, came to the family's assistance. He stormed into the ABC Bank's Oxford Street branch and slammed down on the manager's desk the cash that Georgi was in arrears plus another 6 months repayments. He told the very frightened manager to tell those heartless bastards hounding Georgi and the family "to call off the dogs". They did and the family hurried to get the restaurant finished and up and running again.

At one Sunday evening family dinner when the restaurant was all but completed, someone raised the possibility of the arsonists returning.

Demetios simply muttered "They won't. He, who sent them, is dead." "How do you know that?" they all asked in unison. Demetios just shrugged and muttered, "It was as God willed" and would say no more.

Effie, one of Georgi's sisters recalled after Demetios had gone home that there had been a recent TV report of a prominent western suburbs businessman and developer being beheaded in his penthouse apartment. Police were mystified as to how the killer had gained access to the apartment in view of the heavy security arrangements. Security cameras showed nothing untoward, and police had called for anyone having information to contact them. In view of the manner of the murder, it was believed the killer was of middle eastern origin.

Photos of the murdered man confirmed that he was one and the same as the man who had confronted Georgi. The family, of course, could not be certain that Demetios was the killer, and they were certainly not going to raise their suspicions with the authorities.

Demetios never raised the matter again and neither did the family, but they did wonder.

They were never troubled again. The restaurant came back bigger and better than ever.

The family including Paulos and Demetios lived contentedly together for many years thereafter.

Georgi and Maria remained happily married and ran the Ithaka until they retired. Their elder son (of three) took over the running.

Paulos was the acknowledged leader of the local Greek community. With their encouragement he entered local government politics and subsequently served over many years on the local Council including several terms as Mayor. He was a proud recipient of the Order of Australia Medal for services to the community.

Demetios came to public notice when his portrait by a young Australian born Greek artist received favourable comment at the Annual Archibald Prize competition.

A television executive intrigued by his appearance went to meet him at the restaurant. With his formidable walrus moustached appearance and his pungent gnomic comment, he perceived Demetios as a potential TV personality.

He was right. Demetios was a commanding figure. He did not prattle but his pithy down to earth comment on a morning Panel Show brought much common sense to the program. His Legion background was leaked and this together with his occasional quote from the Q'ran enhanced his persona as someone exotic and exciting. He developed a big following particularly among middle eastern viewers. But it did not change him. He continued to work at the Ithaka and live in his granny flat. He was loyal and committed to the family until he died.

Nic and Mimi died within a few months of one another aged in their eighties. They were much loved by the family having seen it prosper and all the kids do well in the professional and commercial worlds. In their memory, the family established a university scholarship for young people from St. Spyridon's parish.

In his old age, Georgi would take his grand kids into the lounge room after the Sunday evening family dinner and teach them to play cards. The kids always begged to hear his stories of the old uncles on Ithaka and how he beat the casino. Yes, Georgi reflected, those were the days.

BRYN O'TOOLE - THE LUCKIEST MAN

The Long Arm of Coincidence

During the 1970's one of the lurks and perks for NSW Admin staff was getting picked for the migrant ship business acquisition teams.

What this involved was that a small three-man team would fly to Fremantle and board one of the many migrant ships coming to Australia from Europe. The team would work hard during the day opening new accounts and talking to people about home loans. However, at night there was a lot of drinking since alcohol was duty free and very cheap. The younger Flite went on a couple of these trips but was not one of the regulars.

One of his mates Bryn O'Toole was. He and Flite had both worked together in the Treasury area. They had gravitated towards one another and had become firm friends and drinking mates. They had got into and out of a few scrapes together (such as leaving a briefcase containing confidential files in a notorious drinking hole after one heavy Friday night).

Bryn was involved in the Bank's entry into the short-term money market, and they were working closely together in the General Section of the Bank's Head Office. This was a low-profile group, but they were the Bank's general investigative team and possessed considerable clout.

One morning Bryn turned up in the section about 10.30am after returning from one of these migrant ship trips. He looked awful and was very grey around the gills. He and Flite went out into the stairwell so that they could talk privately.

Bryn told his story. He and his two-man team had got off the ship in Melbourne to have a drink with people from one of the Victorian based banks who sometimes “shared” a ship with them. Unfortunately, they overstayed and could not get a cab back to the wharf.

After Bryn bribed a truck driver, they had arrived at the wharf only to see the ship 100 yards out and starting to steam full ahead for the entrance to Port Phillip Bay. The ship was heading to Sydney with their bank cash and new business documents without them. They had to get back on board.

Bryn and his two other team members jumped into a lighter standing by the wharf (after he paid out some more money) and went after the ship which was starting to pick up speed.

There were two other extenuating factors. The first was that Bryn had been given English pounds by the purser to change to US dollars at a good rate. He had done the deal and had the $15,000 in a money belt. The ship’s purser understandably was frantic and could be seen on deck shaking his fist in anger.

The second was that Port Phillip Bay is notorious for sudden storms and if things could not get worse, they soon did with the advent of a windstorm with violent squalls and rough seas. It was especially important then from a safety viewpoint that the ship did not miss the high tide.

There is little doubt that it was a traumatic time. The lighter was able to get alongside the ship which had slowed down a little at the purser’s insistence but was still going fast to get the tide. The purser let down a basket on a line and got his money. He left the deck and could not care less about what happened next.

During a lull, Bryn’s two team members scrambled up a rope ladder and got back on board.

The storm got worse and there was Bryn still in the lighter. Things were getting very dangerous with the ship now steaming full ahead and the lighter trying to keep up with it and constantly crashing against its side.

The lighter man told Bryn in no uncertain terms that things were getting too dangerous for him, and he was going to break away. If he wanted to get on board, he should jump now, adding that he needed to be careful otherwise he could end up between the lighter and the ship.

Bryn jumped and whilst he did initially slip down, the lighter man had the nous to immediately move away from the ships side.

On board, Bryn had to front up to the captain who was furious. He raved and ranted telling him he had put the ship at risk. He banged the table and shouted that "the ABC Bank would never be allowed on board another of the Line's ships."

The loss of this business would have been regarded very seriously by Bank management and it was understandable that Bryn was worried. To calm him down and get him thinking straight, Flite took him down the back stairs to a nearby pub. They talked long and hard about what to do and eventually agreed that the best thing was to say nothing and see what develops.

It was a worrying time, but the luck of the Irish held and as weeks went past, it seemed nothing would come of it. Eventually they learned that the ship's captain had committed suicide on the voyage from Sydney to San Francisco. With so much going on about that, nothing came out about the Bank team missing the ship.

It all went quiet. Bryn worked on the entry into the Money Market and life for Flite went on, chasing bad people.

Some ten years later, Flite and his wife Judy were on a cruise to Asia, Singapore, Hong Kong, and some Japanese coastal cities. The last port of call was Nagasaki (where they dropped the bomb).

As the ship was leaving port and the passengers were lining the decks, two kamikaze cabs raced down to the wharf with six passengers who had missed the boat. They jumped into a lighter and got back on board without any problem.

Flite commented to his wife that the situation was not unlike what happened to Bryn in Melbourne. She was aware of what he was talking about.

By one of the wildest ever coincidences, a woman standing alongside Flite with her husband turned and asked, "Are you talking about the ABC Bank boys who missed a boat in Melbourne years ago?" When Flite confirmed he was, the woman said, "Well I was there, and I have photos of them getting back on board!"

Certainly, a possibility in the millions.

When Flite returned to Sydney and got hold of the photos, there was Bryn looking up grim in the lighter. At this stage, he was in London. So, Flite had the photo enlarged (very big and clear) and sent it off in the London bag. He didn't put any note with it but just wrote on the back "gotchayoubugger!"

Nothing happened for a while but some 6 weeks later, Flite received a small parcel containing a pair of Toledo cuff links from Bryn and a note proclaiming him a "proper bastard", for digging up dirt on his mates that had been long buried. Years later they still have a drink together and talk about it. The wildest possible coincidence surely!

I guess one never knows when some incident you prefer to forget will come back to haunt you!

(This base tale is absolutely true!
The most remarkable coincidence)

SANDY MONTAGU

Who got in and out of trouble

The Montagu family has a long distinguished aristocratic background. For hundreds of years, they exercised a prominent role within English society.

Members of the family were among the earliest settlers to the then new colony of Victoria. They prospered and are numbered among the wealthiest families in Australia. They have extensive holdings in the best sheep and wheat country in both Victoria and New South Wales as well as a strong involvement in the local wine industry.

They mix socially with the Toorak elite and dabble when it suits them in local politics.

Percival (Sandy) Montagu was the eldest son of the family. Like his grandfather and father before him he was educated at the prestigious Scotch College in Melbourne. He rowed in the College champion eight for his year and represented in the college's first XV rugby team. He did reasonably well academically and held a position in the top half of his form. He was a very popular and well-regarded member of his cohort.

After he left school he worked as a jackeroo for a couple years on their farms and loved the life.

His father, however, decided he needed some commercial experience to round him off so that he would be prepared to run things when he stepped down. He arranged for young Sandy to join one of the top accounting firms in Melbourne and to start an accountancy course.

It didn't work. Sandy had some inheritance money and spent most of his time at the local stock exchange, buying and selling shares successfully. He made money and came to realise he was a natural trader with the ability to recognise and seize opportunities.

In the light of this, it would have been better if his father had arranged for him to join a stock-broking firm. He had plenty of contacts with the right people, but he didn't.

His father considered a stint in commercial banking might provide Sandy with some business nous. However, rather than getting him in to one of the big private Banks he chose the small ABC Bank where one of his closest friends, Chairman of a national wool firm was a Board member.

So, Sandy Montagu joined the Bank in Melbourne. Simon Sinclair the then state manager "got the message" and appointed Sandy for his first two years as a member of his personal staff. He was subsequently attached as a supernumerary to branches and given special training in banking practice and lending.

With his family influence and elite school background Sandy was an arrogant, selfish young man. He was full of himself, knew everything and held himself aloof from his banking colleagues. He was pushy and insensitive to the feelings of others.

At 33, he was given his first branch in the state's wheat growing area. Staff were handpicked and very experienced. Of course, he did well. He worked hard at gaining new business and his past ability to recognise opportunity came to the fore. He had the support to clean up after him and to ensure documentation and records were properly maintained. In due course, he was visited by an inspection and audit team to examine branch performance. He got a clean report but made no acknowledgment or expression of thanks to his staff.

He was subsequently promoted to one of the state's largest rural branches. Again, he received special support not extended to others and exceeded Simon's expectations.

Simon meanwhile had been promoted to State Manager NSW. Whilst not particularly smart, Simon had the sense to surround himself with good people to support him. Following his initial visitation of his rural branches, he was far from impressed with the calibre of the managers, many of whom were old, inactive and lacking any real drive.

He needed some catalyst to reinvigorate them, some role model that he could parade and reignite their competitive spirit. Yes, Sandy was the man.

Simon arranged for him to be promoted to a rural branch in South Western New South Wales in a good agricultural, primarily wheat area. The branch in question was Coolong and while it was always considered to have potential, it never performed to expectations.

Simon Sinclair had high hopes that Sandy could show how it should be done. Again, staff calibre was improved, and a well experienced loans officer added to staff numbers as a super-numerary.

Sandy's father flew him, his wife and two young daughters to Coolong in the family Cessna. When they visited the manager's house they were appalled. Sandy's father telephoned Simon and told him that he would not have his son and family living in such a hovel. Following a call from the family friend Board member, the Bank bought a newly renovated Queenslander style home for Sandy some 10 minutes' drive from town.

As expected, when Sandy took up duty, he hit the ground running. He had already met the town's notables and the branch's best clients at his welcome function. He had been given a well experienced and strong second officer to ensure the branch was run efficiently leaving him virtually free to seek new business.

Each morning he would leave the branch after it opened and drive with his supernumerary loans officer to visit his clients and to discuss their financial needs. As he did the rounds, he realised the countryside was very similar to that where his last branch was situated. Crop yields were similar also. Nonetheless property values were only about two thirds of that prevailing in Western Victoria.

Sandy immediately saw the opportunity to make his mark.

Whereas a property might presently be valued for security purposes at $1,000,000, Sandy valued it at $1,500,000. On bank security margins of 66%, the farmer could thus borrow $1,000,000 in lieu of $666,000 subject of course to his income being sufficient to service this.

Sandy spoke informally to the Director of the Regional Government Agricultural Authority one evening at the golf club. He agreed that rainfall over the past ten years had been very good and MIGHT in fact, be the norm because of climate change. The conversation finished there. The Director made no reference regarding longer term patterns. Sandy made no formal enquiry seeking regional rainfall data.

A few of the older farmer hard-heads were sceptical and advised caution. However, most of their colleagues didn't think twice and jumped on the bandwagon. They bought new cars and utes, paid outstanding school fees and the wives went on long delayed shopping sprees in Sydney and Melbourne. Farming equipment sales boomed and most of the town's unemployed who wanted to work got employment.

The word got around, and people flew in from all over to get some of this "cheap" land.

Things went well for some three years but then along came a prolonged drought. Both the johnny-come-latelys and local farmers who had benefitted from inflated valuations came to the reality. Certainly, rainfall over recent years had been wonderful. However, when you looked at the 100-year pattern the average rainfall was substantially below that.

The reality was that the area experienced prolonged droughts on a regular basis, a factor which manifested itself in the earlier lower property values existing when Sandy Montagu first turned up on the scene. His higher valuations had been based on the false premise of higher rainfall.

The Bank found itself with some forty clients with debts of a million or more where they were fully exposed and not protected by their normal margin of unlent value in the security property (i.e. the difference between the amount of loan and the real value of property).

The Bank, of course, was not faced with immediate loss. This would occur if it had to sell up a farmer and they did not achieve a price greater than their loan. In the light of this, it was essential that the farms should continue to be worked and maintained as going concerns.

The last thing the Bank would want was the farmer to give up and walk off the land recognising he had no equity in it. Common-sense fortunately prevailed. Whilst not accepting any blame the Bank relented to the extent of reducing interest rates and allowing principal repayment holidays for a few years. They treated sympathetically any farmer who was experiencing financial hardship.

The drought was followed by several good years and prices. Slowly debts reduced and realistic prices for agricultural land rose. With this, the Bank's over-exposure gradually diminished, and it became more comfortable with its situation.

Nevertheless, the branch was a basket case for some 10 years. Not surprisingly, most of the farmers in question as soon as they were able took their business elsewhere.

Sandy as soon as he saw the writing on the wall resigned never to return to the town again.

His father fully aware of Sandy's role in the fiasco shunted him off to the family's new wheat farm at the Esperance in Western Australia.

Simon Sinclair was caught in the middle. On one hand he had to explain what went wrong but bearing in mind the board member's relationship with the family, he could not place too much blame on Sandy.

With the connivance of the Bank's Chief Valuer, he concocted a convincing story of being inadvertently misled by government agency advice as to the true state of rainfall and that the past 10-year experience could now be typical.

When Sandy went to Esperance he found that the family's interests were being well looked after by their local manager and he really had nothing much to do. He started to look around for other opportunities to fill in his time.

During the 1980s there was considerable interest in nickel mining in the West and there was a lot of exploration and claims of finding rich deposits.

Esperance was "too small" for Sandy and his wife, and they decided to live in Dalkeith, a trendy suburb of Perth. With his polo playing prowess and obvious wealthy background, he was soon ensconced among the upper echelons of Perth society.

Esperance was some 600km from Perth and usually he would fly his Cessna over from Perth spending usually three days on family company management and other affairs and then flying home.

Many of those with whom Sandy mixed socially were deeply involved in mining investment and its governance. They had access to insider information that was not available to the public at large.

Many of his close associates had made fortunes in the notorious Poseidon Nickel Bubble where $1 shares in the venture increased rapidly on exaggerated expectations to a peak of $282 but quickly declined when the bubble burst.

With the nickel mining boom continuing and access to the right information, Sandy rediscovered his former capabilities and became a highly successful trader in mining stocks.

One of his new friends mentioned that his father was putting together a small syndicate of family friends (all members of the wealthiest and powerful families in the west) to acquire an existing nickel mine.

The mine was being sold due to the death of the principal shareholder and managing director who had been a close friend of three or four of the syndicate members including Sandy's friend's father. The mine was operating profitably, and assay confirmed the lease had strong potential.

The site was in barren god-forbidden country not far from the notorious Poseidon nickel mine which was still in full operation and operating profitably.

Sandy's earlier share trading had increased his grandmother's inheritance to nearly $400,000. He invested all but $100,000 of this with the syndicate. Sandy was still receiving a handsome annual salary from the family business and the subsequent return from the mine investment proved to be a welcome addition to his income.

Things went well for some three years; mine output was good and there were no industrial problems. World ore prices fluctuated somewhat but not to the extent to significantly impact adversely on profitability.

Then things changed. The ore lode began to thin out and production fell to about half of recent past output. The mine's financial viability was also exacerbated by a sharp decline in the world nickel price. Other small mines nearby started to close and placed on a "maintenance" basis so that operations could recommence when prices rose sufficiently.

Sandy's group tried to hold on but as time went by operations became increasingly unprofitable and closure became inevitable.

When this occurred, the Bank who had lent the company $1.5 million when the mine was purchased to acquire new equipment and undertake needed refurbishment, called their loan in.

Sandy was required to come up with $150,000 as his share of the bank debt. He had sold the major portion of his share portfolio to buy into the mine syndicate and this call could not have come at a worse time. The devastating October 1987 Black Tuesday when share markets worldwide had crashed had occurred only a couple of weeks earlier. Sandy lost heavily when he sold the few shares he had left.

He was faced with a shortfall of $100,000.

His home at Dalkeith had been acquired by the family company and was in it's name. He could not borrow the residual amount against it. He, his younger brother and sister had a 49% share of the family agricultural and wine company, worth millions. But again, there was no way he could access this to help him.

His father would not help saying he had got himself into this mess and it was up to him to get out of it. He also made it clear that he believed Sandy was accident prone and could not be trusted in a management role. Sandy could no longer aspire to managing the family estate after he died, and he would in future groom Sandy's younger brother to do so.

Sandy was in the pits and did not know which way to turn. His world was fast falling apart.

A syndicate member, learning of Sandy's plight, offered to buy his 300,000 $1 fully paid shares in the mine for $150,000. He was tempted but stubbornly declined the offer. A nearby company also made an offer for the mine but well below the syndicate's purchase price. This too was declined.

Sandy's wife Peta was the daughter of a senior partner in one of Melbourne's oldest and most prestigious law firms. He and Peta had been married for some ten years. They had two young daughters and while he still loved her it did not stop him from having a dalliance or two with other women.

Peta was aware of his loss on the share market, but he had not told her about the Bank call. She was a social butterfly, had always been used to wealth and had been spoilt and cosseted by her parents. Sandy similarly lavished upon her anything she wished for.

Sandy had been moping around the house for several days and was obviously deeply worried about something. While having their usual drink before dinner, Peta asked Sandy what was bothering him and making him miserable.

When he told he had to find $100,000, she laughed and said, "Is that all, I thought it was something serious like you had prostate cancer!"

Peta went on "Don't you know I have money; I can give it to you!"

Sandy said, "But it is $100,000." Peta laughed and said "I told you I have money and in fact, I think it is some $300,000. You can have what you need!"

It turns out that years ago her mother's brother who had been a wealthy Victorian grazier had died and left his two nieces $250,000 each. He had never married and regarded these kids as his own.

Peta went on to tell Sandy that the money had been held on term deposit in the bank ever since and she had never touched it. Both her parents and Sandy had always given her anything she wanted.

In the intervening years, the funds through compound interest had grown and now there was a need for it, she was happy to let Sandy have whatever he wanted. Sandy could not believe his good fortune not only for the unexpected windfall but that he had such a wife.

With the Bank repaid and the mine in mothballs, the syndicate just bided its time waiting for something to happen.

There was, however, one exception, the syndicate's mining engineer. He was mystified by the diminishing quality of ore extracted in the light of the original exploration assay results. Up to this stage, the mine tunnelling was heading westward towards the Poseidon workings.

On a whim, he went to the mine with a couple of men and started tunnelling halfway along but in a northerly direction. When they came to a rock face, they drilled holes and set explosives. On the surface, they set them off. It was one almighty bang and they had obviously used too much explosive. After the dust and smoke settled, they ventured back inside. In places, parts of the roof had come down but it all still seemed safe enough.

When they got to the site of the blast, a cavity had been created some two and half metres wide by three metres high.

What was exciting though was that in the light from their lamps there were a multitude of glints, shiny stuff in the debris of fallen rock ….. gold! The blast had uncovered what appeared to be a significant vein of the stuff.

They sat down in disbelief.

There had been a similar occurrence a couple of years earlier at a mine to the northwest. In that case, they had struck a once in a lifetime mother lode. This was a similar happening.

The engineer excitedly contacted the head of the syndicate to relate the good news. This new find turned out to be a bonanza with syndicate members receiving more than four times their investment over the next five years. After that, whilst the mine continued to produce, the quality of ore gradually reduced. Some three years later operations ceased.

Following Peta's ready financial assistance that got him off the hook Sandy reflected on his life so far. He came to recognise that at Coolong he had been a smart-ass ignoring caution and by rushing in blindly, had caused considerable rancour and distress.

He also regretted his infidelities that, if revealed, would have caused considerable hurt to Peta and destroyed his family. He had been a bloody fool and his unnecessary aggressive pursuit of wealth to the detriment of all else had blinded him to what should be important in his life.

It was a watershed time for him. He knew he had to change, and he did. From then on, he was no longer the pushy aggro hustler of old and spent the rest of his life living quietly and comfortably, a good family man devoted to Peta and his two daughters.

His brother, whom his father had been grooming to take over from him when he died, drowned tragically when the tractor he was driving on the edge of a dam tipped on soft ground pinning him under the water. His father never got over it.

His father did swallow his pride and offer Sandy the chance of taking over, but he declined.

Ultimately Sandy's sister and her farm overseer husband took over the reins and made a good fist of it. The old man had previously disinherited her because she had married this man, one of their farm employees, ignoring his strong objection.

As it turned out though, the marriage was a godsend and through the input of practical experience and knowledge of the husband, the Montagu farming operation survived and prospered.

The old man was bitter to the end, never acknowledging his son-in-law or his part in their continuing prosperity. He never spoke to Sandy after he declined to come back to run things. He died a lonely, extremely unhappy man.

As for the Bank's branch at Coolong, its business base stagnated and years later still had a bad name in the town. Country people have long memories!

Simon Sinclair could not really come to terms with the fact that his judgement had let him down. He knew his explanation, placing the blame elsewhere was a straight out lie and would be readily exposed if any serious enquiries were made. But none were.

He was high enough up the hierarchical ladder to be among the Bank's most senior people. The members of this "club" invariably stuck together to protect one another as far as they could. The last thing they wanted was some wildfire controversy that might incite wider questions from the Board and expose them all to scrutiny. Accordingly, when potential problems of this kind arose, the safest ploy was to sweep it under the carpet. And they did.

And so, Simon got out of gaol. A confirmation of the old story that the higher up the ladder you are, the better your chances are of getting away with just about anything.

HISTORICAL NOTE

Lord Chelmsford - Defeat of British Army by Zulus Isandlwana South Africa 1879

Source: Author unknown and undated - Article: wikipedia.com

In 1874, Sir Henry Bartle Frere was sent to South Africa by the British Government to consolidate the various diverse groups some of British stock as well as the Boers and Zulus into a federation.

Whilst not stated, the real aim of British Imperial interests was to bring about rule by the white minority over the largely black populace and the establishment of a large pool of cheap labour to work their plantations and mines.

The various groups were not blind to the British real intentions and Frere experienced great difficulty in convincing those groups with no allegiance to the British Crown as to the merits of federation. The Boers refused outright. The powerful Zulu nation were also strongly averse to the idea.

Frustrated by the latter's refusal, Frere lost patience and following rejection of an ultimatum, he called on Lord Chelmsford who was commanding British forces in South Africa to invade their territory (action that had been previously vetoed by the British Government).

Chelmsford had a poor opinion of indigenous warriors from earlier battle experience against the Xhosa tribe, a belief that would lead to dire consequences. The Zulu, however, were a far different kettle of fish, brave, well disciplined, and confident of their prowess.

Chelmsford foolishly split his troops and sent his central column numbering some 1800 men together with civilians and native auxiliaries forward into Zulu country.

A few days later 22 January 1879, they were ambushed at a place called Isandlwana by some twenty-four thousand Zulu warriors armed only with metal tipped thrusting spear-assegais and raw hide shields.

The British infantry attempted to hold back the wave after wave of impis in their normal linear fashion (the famous thin red line) with concentrated volley fire from their modern breech loading martini-henry rifle.

These battle tactics had always sustained them well in the past.

However, the army had been split and the resulting fire power of this smaller group (devoid also of quick firing gatling guns) was commensurately reduced. It proved insufficient to hold off the vast numbers attacking them and they were overrun. In the ensuing debacle, 1,300 British troops were massacred.

When it was known that the force was under attack, Chelmsford had specifically ordered that a possible relief force nearby should stay where it was and not render assistance.

When the British public learned of the defeat, the worst they had ever suffered in Africa and exacerbated too by the fact that they had been beaten by a "bunch of savages", there was a huge outcry.

With this great wave of anger came strident furious calls for Chelmsford's recall. He regained some of his tarnished military reputation when with a strongly reinforced army (including gatling guns) he soundly defeated the Zulus six months later at Ulundi and sent their king into exile.

Nevertheless, the ground swell for his recall continued and Disraeli the British prime minister and his cabinet were under increasing pressure to accede to the public's wishes.

He was prevented from doing so by Queen Victoria. Chelmsford was a favourite of hers and whenever Disraeli raised the possibility of recall she would stoutly defend him and refuse to sanction any such action.

Chelmsford had told the Queen that the defeat was due to the disobedience of the commanding officer, Colonel Durnford in not establishing a defensive position by entrenchment and the laagering the supply wagons, as ordered.

The subsequent military enquiry, however, could find no evidence that the order had ever issued. Even if it had, it would have proven impractical to carry out due to the suddenness and surprise of the attack.

Following his victory at Ulrundi which virtually ended Zulu resistance, Chelmsford was replaced.

When he returned to Britain, the defeat was investigated by an Army tribunal. Whilst he was seriously censured, he kept his rank but would never again serve in the field.

In the normal course, one might have expected that with this indictment and the damage done to British prestige, he would have been persona non grata to those at the highest levels of British society. This was not the case.

Notwithstanding the Army censure, he was honoured soon afterwards by the Queen by being awarded the Knight Grand Cross of Bath. But it did not end there.

For the next twenty years until he died, he continued to be favoured being promoted to lieutenant general in 1882, Lieutenant of the Tower of London (1884 until 1889), colonel of the 4th (West London) Rifle Volunteer Corps (1887), full general (1888), and colonel of the Derbyshire Regiment (1889). He exchanged the colonelcy of the Derbyshires for that of the 2nd Life Guards (1900), and as such was Gold Stick in Waiting during ceremonial events at Court. King Edward VII appointed him Knight Grand Cross of the Royal Victorian Order (GCVO) in the November 1902 Birthday Honours list.

Quite a remarkable subsequent career in view of the circumstances!

Reflecting on all that occurred, one can only acknowledge the cynical truth that the higher up the status ladder one is, the better your chances are of getting away with a catastrophic defeat (or blame for a financial disaster).

It is apparent that this is true today as it was then!

A MISTAKEN MAN

Note and Voucher Cancelling Machine 710

The Bank's office machinery and stationery warehouse at Surry Hills was an old double storied warehouse five minutes' walk from Central Station. Whilst current stock of machines and equipment awaiting issue were held in the ground floor area, the first-floor space housed a vast accumulation of obsolete and broken-down items.

Over the years, individual machines and equipment had been written off the books but nothing had ever been gotten rid of in the forlorn hope that one day it might prove useful. It rarely had and now the floor was stacked with all this useless material.

When the long-time manager of the Store retired, and a new man appointed, his first move was to try and get rid of this accumulation and free up space room for his expanding inventory on the now bulging ground floor.

Flite was delegated to arrange disposal.

It was readily agreed that most if not all the stored items in question should be scrapped. Even so, the Bank's Head Office dictated that all machinery to be destroyed must be identified by serial number for possible future reference.

With one exception, this was not a problem as a proper record of all items was held.

The exception was this huge old treadle operated machine that had been used in the past to punch the pinhole word "cancelled" and date on mutilated notes withdrawn from issue and vouchers. No serial number had been recorded.

Thinking it would be an easy task Flite sent one of the junior staff to seek the serial number. He returned very distressed to confess he could not find any identifying number.

Rather than go through the exercise again, Flite contacted the Store Manager and asked if he would get one of his staff to check it out.

The Store Manager subsequently rang back to say his man had had a devil of a time finding anything but finally had found the number 710 on it. He commented "that it was just a question of looking in the right place!!!!!!"

The unit was subsequently scheduled on the Schedule of Office Machinery for Destruction as "Voucher/Note Cancelling Machine serial number 710" and scrapped with the rest.

Later, reflecting on the exercise the realisation suddenly hit Flite like a ton of bricks that 710 was not an identifying number at all.

Rather, it was an indication by the machine's maker of where to OIL the monstrosity.

JIMMY DUNCAN

A Loyal Man

Bill Hansen and Jimmy Duncan were next door neighbours living on the Arncliffe ridge looking down into Botany Bay.

Bill was the Manager of the ABC Bank's Tempe branch 10 minutes' drive from his home.

Jimmy was a maths teacher at the local co-ed high school.

They were great mates, avid St. George Rugby League team supporters. Whenever their team was playing on television on a Sunday afternoon, they would knock off from their gardening or anything else they were doing, don their white, red vee club jerseys and watch the game and sink a few tinnies in the process.

Afterwards they would have a barbeque with their joint families. Invariably, Bill would be brow-beaten by his wife for his ineptitude, not cooking the sausages to her liking, making the barbeque smoke, putting too much dressing on the salad.

She was continually nasty but Bill would just smile and let it pass.

One evening after they had eaten and the kids were playing touch football in the backyard, the parents got to talking about their children and how they were growing up and developing.

They were all doing well with no black cloud hanging over their heads. Their future looked bright.

Jimmy commented that there were other kids who were not so lucky. He mentioned the plight of a girl student in his maths class, a bright young lady but who had been diagnosed with leukaemia. She needed a bone marrow replacement very soon otherwise her life prospects were bleak.

The family had no health cover insurance. The daughter was on the Government Health list for treatment as a public patient, but it seemed she would have to wait some months before she would obtain assistance.

Jim explained that her situation was critical and that if the delay was lengthy, she would be dead before she became eligible for her operation.

Her parents were good, hard working people but battlers and could not raise the $70,000 odd needed for her treatment. They had been to all the big Banks but had been knocked back.

Jimmy asked Bill, “Might you be able to do something?” So, Bill went to see the parents, Doug and Barbara Ellis and met Joanie the young lady with leukemia.

Doug was a storeman for an automotive parts company. Barbara had been a nursing sister but with her sick daughter and two younger sons she had her hands full and was a stay-at-home mum.

They had $6,000 in the Bank but apart from an older car had no other assets. The house they were living in belonged to Barbara’s mother.

Her father, who had been a senior public servant had died some 10 years earlier. Her mother had subsequently put another storey on the house for her own use and had let Barbara and Doug and family live downstairs. They paid no rent but paid council rates, electricity and water bills. It was expected that Doug would undertake any maintenance required.

Unfortunately, the mother had developed dementia 12 months ago and had to move into a nursing home. Under existing arrangements, if they were to be observed, there was no way Bill could help. The Bank’s maximum unsecured loan was $20,000 and a mortgage loan for $70,000 was out of the question as they did not own the house. The mother who did own it, was legally incapable.

It is very important in banking that you always keep your clients at arm's length and do not let your heart rule your head in granting loans. In many cases, the action does not help either the borrower or the lender.

Bill, at heart, was a softie and foolishly let his heart rule his head. He could see that Joanie could well die unless she received treatment very soon. On the hand, he could only help if he broke the Bank's rules but in doing so he would certainly jeopardise his future. After some reflection, he decided to do what he could and face up to the inevitable no matter what it might be, even if it meant the sack.

It is often the case that when people repay their home loan, they leave the certificate of title to their property with the Bank to be held in safe custody. This was the case with Barbara's parents. They had repaid their loan at Tempe branch and the certificate of title was still held there.

And so, Bill contrived a deal.

He would fund a loan of $65,000 (that is, the net amount after funds raised by the school) in names of Doug and Barbara Ellis. He would take a mortgage from them acknowledging the debt over the mother's house property (which they did not own). In essence, it was worthless as a security.

He had sighted and held a copy of the mother's will in which Barbara was named as the sole beneficiary. He could not register the mortgage. However, in so far as he held the certificate of title on naked lodgement, he did hold some leverage.

To further assist the parents, he applied an interest rate at half the going rate. He had no authority to do this. He "doctored" the Bank's internal records to show appropriate (but untrue) detail. He had stuck his neck out and was at serious risk albeit for a good cause.

Joanie successfully underwent her transplant operation with a brother proving to be a compatible donor. She convalesced well and at the end of 12 months was able to return to school.

Two years later, she was third in the state in 4 Unit mathematics in her Higher School Certificate exams. A great result for all concerned, particularly for both Bill and Jimmy.

Jimmy was aware of the risky situation Bill had placed himself in and was deeply concerned for him, particularly as it was he who had first raised Joanie's plight. He had his fingers crossed that things would turn out right.

Some 6 months later, Barbara's mother died, and she inherited the house.

When she and Doug came to the branch to tell Bill the news, he was greatly relieved and told them we can now set things on the straight and narrow again with a normal housing loan. But no, Doug and Barbara wanted to refinance the loan with the Commonwealth Bank whose going rate was a quarter of one percent less than the ABC Bank.

Bill was greatly disappointed that they did not retain some loyalty notwithstanding that he had put himself at great risk in the process and that the extra cost was minimal. As Barbara commented, "It is a matter of principle Bill, your rate is higher!"

Any way about a month later, the refinance settled, and the ABC Bank's debt was extinguished.

But that was not the end. Barbara could not help herself.

Despite Bill's caution never to talk about her deal, she complained to the Manager at the Commonwealth branch approving their refinance loan that the interest rate was much more than what she was paying previously. That of course was an unauthorised special concession that Bill granted them.

The Commonwealth Manager thought it strange and mentioned it to his District Manager. He agreed and telephoned his opposite number in the ABC Bank NSW Admin querying "Are you buggers trying to get under the market? What's the story?"

The ABC Bank's District Manager agreed that it was out of the ordinary and informed Flite who sent an Inspector to investigate. The cat came out of the bag and Bill's sympathetic but ill-advised actions came to light.

The Bank had missed out on several thousand in interest. He had also been underhand in the dealing, falsified records and technically, put the bank at risk. He was asked to resign. The matter was not reported to the police.

In some way, fulfillment of the adage that no good deed goes unpunished.

When he got home that night with a lot on his mind, as he opened his front gates his car slowly passed him running down the incline to his garage. He had not put on the brakes.

Jumping in just before he hit the garage wall, he put his foot on the brakes only it was the accelerator. He slammed into the exterior wall of the garage and a huge RSJ girder holding up the façade of the house above the garage door crashed down on the bonnet of the car just in front of him.

His wife came running out screaming, "What have you done this time?"

Bill got inside, poured himself a scotch and sat down, shaking with shock. His wife came into the room hysterically calling out, "How did you do that? You are stupid, you can't do anything right! You are a fool."

It was obviously not the appropriate time, but Bill shakily told her he had been sacked and the reason why. His wife exploded, "That's the last straw! I am leaving you. You stupidly put our future at risk for somebody you don't even know. I can't understand you!"

The divorce was ugly. His wife was a legal assistant in a firm specialising in Family Law cases. She bled him dry. He lost his house and ended up living in a caravan at the back of his son's home.

He could not get a clerical job anywhere and ended up as a "lolly-pop" man in a Council road team. His mate Jimmy stuck by him and regularly came by for a chat and a beer.

His life focussed on his son's young kids and their progress in life. In all other respects he was shattered emotionally and started losing interest in things, even the St. George rugby league club. He arrived at the state of mind, that his life was not worth living.

One Sunday night about 10pm, he drove out in his old Holden to The Gap at Watsons Bay, a place notorious for people wanting to suicide by jumping from the cliff face to the surf and rocks below.

He sat down for a while listening to the sound of the surf, thinking about his life and its present futility. His reverie, such as it was, was interrupted by a couple of young men from the local Baptist Church.

They and some of their colleagues regularly visited the spot particularly on a Sunday evening when suicides occur more frequently to talk to any potential jumper. They had a thermos of coffee and over a cup talked to a very confused Bill.

He really didn't know why he was there. Perhaps he would have jumped. He wasn't sure. After a while he seemed to come to his senses. He thanked the two young fellows, drove home and had a good night's sleep. He had crossed an emotional threshold and was now more settled and reconciled to his circumstances. He didn't miss the Bank and began to enjoy the freedom of his job on the road and the camaraderie of his work mates.

One Saturday morning he was having a late lie-in when his son called out from the back door that there was someone here to see him. Hastily donning a pair of shorts and tee shirt he walked into the house to the front door. It was jimmy looking the worst for wear. He told Bill that he thought he should come over and have a beer with him. Bill replied that it was only just 10am and a bit early.

Anyway, when they sat down in the caravan and took the top off a couple of Stellas, Jimmy broke the news. Bill had been in a Lotto Syndicate at Jimmy's school but after he got the sack from the Bank he had dropped out.

Jimmy recognising his own part in Bill's fall from grace had continued to pay his fortnightly contribution to the syndicate.

Jimmy now told an incredulous Bill that their ship had just come in, their syndicate of 10 members sharing a win of $30 million. Bill was now richer to the extent of $3 million.

How things changed!

It is always said that "one good turn deserves another" and so it was for Bill. He could not believe his luck after his past misfortunes. He paid off his son's house mortgage and gave him another hundred thousand to help him and his family. He made a sizeable donation to the Baptist Church at Watsons Bay.

Then Bill and Jimmy and his wife bought a pub up on the far north coast of New South Wales and spent the life of larry from then on enjoying all the good things and their mateship.

Bill never married again but he did learn to surf good!

RICK RYAN

A Badly Done-by Man

When you are dealing in money there is always the risk of someone with "sticky" fingers getting their hands on it. Understandably, Banks have strict rules for staff handling and securing of raw cash.

Not surprisingly, they also expect staff to handle their personal affairs in a proper manner avoiding gambling or other behaviour that might lead them into error.

When sizeable amounts of cash go missing, their investigations are very thorough with special focus on determining whether a rogue staff member is involved. They probe into the private and financial affairs of all staff (perusing bank accounts for indications of gambling) and encouraging individuals to divulge the "dirt" on their colleagues.

When these events occur, it is not a happy time for staff and the camaraderie that might once have existed disappears forever. Individuals directly involved are sometimes traumatised for a long time.

One such case happened at a large suburban branch (before decimal currency was introduced).

Teller 1 at the branch was Rick Ryan, a young married man with a baby due in a couple of months. He was a quiet man, conscientious and popular among his colleagues.

The branch was in the centre of an industrial area with many business firms banking with it.

Rick as Teller 1 only dealt with business clients. It was an onerous job involving receipt of substantial cash and cheque deposits but in those days before payroll services, also making large cash cheque payouts with complex note specifications.

The telling line was a busy one particularly on Friday and at close of business that day, Rick's cash drawers were generally awash. On such occasions, the branch accountant would direct a senior person to help Rick count his cash and facilitate his balance.

Rick had been on the lower telling line for the best part of two years previously and had never recorded a discrepancy. His good record crashed when some three weeks apart, he ended up firstly fifty pounds then one hundred pounds short. Investigations to identify the deficiencies were unsuccessful. Rick was counselled and warned against any future shortages.

If things were going bad for him, they were going to get worse.

On a Friday, a couple of months later, he reported he was five hundred pounds short. Again, efforts to identify the discrepancy were unsuccessful.

In those times, this was not an inconsiderable figure, and the Bank was seriously concerned. The Bank's Head Office despatched an inspection team of hard-nosed officers to investigate, led by a Senior Inspector.

These individuals interrogated all staff in turn from the Manager down to the junior female typiste. They scrutinised staff bank accounts looking for indications of financial hardship or undesirable habits and delved into personal lives for evidence of misconduct or devious behaviour.

They uncovered that the Corporate Services Supervisor worked as a penciller for a rails-bookmaker on weekends: another confessed to a gambling habit and owed three hundred pounds to his SP bookmaker. He had nothing in his account and was living from payday to payday.

The Corporate Services Supervisor was bluntly told to give up his weekend job or face the sack. He did.

Under intense questioning by the Senior Inspector about his finances and their possible linkage to Rick Ryan's shortages, the staff member with gambling debts finally broke and confessed to stealing the fifty pounds and hundred pounds when helping him. He denied having anything to do with the missing five hundred pounds.

The Inspector demanded his immediate resignation. Having signed this, he was marched out the door. His parents repaid the one hundred and fifty pounds. The matter was not reported to the police.

During such investigations, it occasionally happens that embarrassing private behaviour is disclosed with dire consequences.

In one other case during this investigation, scrutiny of one young teller's account showed a regular series of cheque encashments at a gymnasium and massage establishment well known as a gay brothel. When confronted, the young man was devastated and highly embarrassed. In those times, there was no tolerance of gay people. The Inspector told him he constituted a risk because of potential blackmail and sacked him on the spot. The young man in tears signed his resignation and went home.

When he told his parents of his resignation and the reason for it, his strait-laced church going parents were horrified and ashamed. He received no solace or sympathy but was disowned, told to get out and leave home and never come back.

The next day, the poor young man was tragically found, hanging from a tree in the Queens Park Reserve.

It certainly was a traumatic emotionally searing period for the branch staff. The inspection team were also frustrated in that their investigation was unsuccessful.

They could not break Rick Ryan who continually protested his innocence of any wrongdoing. He was transferred to another branch and his record marked that he should never in future be allowed control of cash. He remained emotionally scarred by the rough treatment he had endured at the hands of the Investigating Inspector.

Rick spent the next 25 years working as a general hand mostly in the lending field at different branches. He never received any recognition by way of promotion and all in all, with the blot on his name, it was very soul destroying. Nevertheless, he remained outwardly cheerful and continued to work conscientiously.

In the mid-1980s, he was working as a conveyancer in the State Admin's Branch Conveyancing section. On a couple of occasions, his section head, Nick Papadakis approached Flite to get a promotion for him. On each occasion, the request backed by Simon Sinclair was rejected by the Human Resources Inspector.

Over the years, the Bank's corporate business base grew substantially and many branch premises particularly those serving industrial areas were proving too small. This was the case at the branch where the five hundred pounds went missing and renovations were proposed. The loans section at one end of the banking chamber was moved upstairs to the unused Manager's residence. With this section gone, it was planned to re-configure the counter and provide more space for general staff where they had vacated.

The remodelling of the counter took place over the October long weekend. Two senior staff were deputised to be present whilst builders were at work in the office. A big work team started at 7am on the Saturday and immediately got to work dismantling the counter.

It soon became evident that the counter had been reconstructed previously but without removal of much of the original 50-year construction. The new counter being installed consisted of several prefabricated units and a new façade. In the light of this, the whole of the existing counter including the original construction had to be done away with.

The original counter had been strongly constructed with plenty of timber and this made the job of dismantling more difficult than originally envisaged. After the top of the counter had been removed, the existing façade followed.

As they removed the last portion where Rick's teller box had been, there was a splash of colour and there in the debris lay two piles of notes, blue coloured five-pound notes and orange ten shilling notes. The rubber bands originally holding the bundles together had perished and when the notes had hit the floor they had spilled and spread. The mystery of Rick's deficiency was solved.

Rick's cash drawer on the day had been overflowing and this bundle of five pound notes had been caught when the drawer was closed and been forced over the back to lodge on a hidden ledge beneath.

The teller's box had been well and truly searched but the ledge in question had been formed when previous remodelling of the original counter had been carried out. People looking into the teller's box under the cash drawers would only have seen the back of this work, the ledge with the notes was well and truly hidden. After all this time, some 25 odd years, Rick was at long last vindicated.

Simon Sinclair called Rick to his office and broke the news to him. He sat down and wept. Through tears, he recounted how he had carried this cross on his back for years always unsure whether people trusted him. To his credit, Simon quickly reported matters to Head Office and was successful in gaining a two-grade promotion for Rick, now designated Senior Conveyancing Officer.

Nonetheless, amply demonstrating their real indifference, he never received any congratulatory response from the Bank's upper echelons on his vindication. Nonetheless he remained a contented, happier man for the rest of his time with the Bank until he retired.

The Inspector who headed the investigation (known disparagingly as "008") continued in this role for several years. He was a bumbling fool and notably unsuccessful in uncovering perpetrators of staff fraud. However, with his harsh bullying, which was never reined in, he left behind a trail of misery. He never contacted Rick.

It perhaps says something about the man that on the day he retired from the Bank (and received his superannuation payout) his wife left him!

The small, odd bundle of twenty pounds in 10 shilling notes was a mystery. It apparently had lain on the hidden ledge for some time. Some teller in the past had obviously been twenty pounds short and like Rick had never known why.

TWO FORGETFUL MEN

The Bank employed Guardian Security Services both for selected property security such as after-hours surveillance, alarm monitoring and as a secure cash provider.

The company used a fleet of armoured vans to deliver cash ordered by branches to replenish their holdings. Each van might make several visits to different sites on its daily run.

After cash had been ordered, the company's van would call at the branch at random times to avoid a regular practice that might prove advantageous for criminals planning an attack. Two-armed security men would alight from the van carrying the cash ordered in a locked bag and enter the office. Inside, at some convenient spot, the cash would be handed over to the treasury custodians, the amount verified in bulk by counting bundles and signed for. The security men would then leave taking with them any surplus notes and coin surplus to requirements.

It was constantly stressed to staff that cash, any cash, should not be left unsecured, unattended. A mandatory direction that especially applied to cash deliveries. Such cash, invariably a large amount, was never to be left but verified by count and secured in the branch treasury cash safe as expeditiously as possible.

Notwithstanding such warnings, too much exposure sometimes led to a weakening in the necessary care.

Johnstown (formerly St John's Town) was an older semi-industrial inner-city suburb of Sydney on the Princes Highway running south. Its name derived from the old stone Anglican church, St. John's a bit further down the highway.

The Bank's branch was a small six hander.

On the day in question the branch had ordered a delivery of some thirty thousand made up of three different denominations.

The Johnstown branch delivery was the van's last call for the day and took place just before 3pm. Normally the exchange would have taken place in the Manager's office. However, the Loans Officer was conducting an interview there with a young couple applying for a home loan. In view of this, the hand-over took place in the staff luncheon room. The luncheon period was well and truly over, and it was unlikely that staff had any need to enter there.

So before returning to his office to talk to the young couple, the Manager picked up the cash bundles and placed them on the kitchen bench putting a tea towel over them. Closing and locking the door behind them, he said to the Accountant, "After I finish inside, we will count it and get it into the safe."

Both were busy for the rest of the day with the normal tasks of their job. They totally forgot all about the cash delivery on the kitchen bench and went home.

Early next morning around 4:30am, the forgetful Manager sat bolt upright in bed aghast. The cash delivery!!!!!!! Worried sick, he hurriedly dressed and drove to the branch some 25 minutes away.

He parked in the area behind the branch and tried to fit his key into the door to open it. Fumbling with worry, he finally opened the door and rushed inside, turned off the alarm and strode into the staff luncheon room. The previously locked door was open, and its key hung on its hook in the door's timber frame.

The unbarred window at the end of the room, admittedly some 10 feet off the ground was slightly ajar. But waves of anguish ran through him as he realised the cash bundles were gone.

God! What was he to do?

Perhaps the Accountant had realised the cash had not been put away and had come in and put it away somewhere safe. Thinking about it, no he would not have done that without ringing me.

Perhaps someone had got in through window (which was probably shut but not locked) and taken the money. But then there was the security alarm that would be triggered off by any movement inside. No, unlikely!

Staff had no reason to go into the lunchroom after 3pm and they would not have known cash was there.

Then the awful thought crossed his mind, perhaps the Accountant had come in earlier and instead of putting it in a safe place, he had taken it and hidden it at home.

Nobody would know!

How was he going to explain it?

He went into his office and rang the Accountant to tell him to come in. He did not explain why at this early hour.

The Accountant realised when driving in that the cash had been left out. As he came into the Manager's office, he laughingly said "How did we forget that???" But when he saw the Manager's face, he quickly realised something was wrong. The Manager blurted out "the bloody money has gone" and put his head down on the desk between his hands.

The Accountant raced out to the staff room and returned white faced. The Manager sat up and said "I am sorry I have to ask this. Did you come in earlier and take it?" The pain this caused the Accountant was obvious. Seriously taken aback he vehemently denied doing it. Then with a momentary flash of survival he retorted, "I could ask you the same question, you could have taken it also. You were here by yourself, the first person in since yesterday." The Manager nodded and agreed but denied he had taken it, saying "it was not enough to flee to South America with."

They just sat there in silence until 9 o'clock when the Manager rang Simon Sinclair to report the loss.

Simon was understandably irate (another mishap he would have to report to Head Office). He told the Manager in no uncertain terms that he and his Accountant had been negligent and that they could easily be sacked. He was sending a Branch Inspector to investigate, and they should render him every assistance.

The Manager then called the staff together and pleaded if anybody knew anything to come forward. Their unanimous response was that they did not know cash was in lunchroom, the door was closed, and no one had reason to go in after lunch.

When they opened for business, there were few customers. One older lady approached the counter wanting to see the Manager but as the Branch Inspector's arrival was imminent, an appointment was made for her at 11:30am.

On the Inspector's arrival, he took the Manager and the Accountant separately into the former's office to recount their version of events from the arrival of the cash delivery until now. Both mentioned that the other had ample opportunity to take the cash.

The Inspector was non-committal throughout but as each one concluded, he paused for about a minute and then asked very roughly, "You have omitted one important detail. What happened to the money?" Both were taken aback, stumbling their words in their hurry to deny any knowledge of it. The Manager pointed out that whilst it was a lot of money it was not enough to warrant stealing and jeopardising one's future.

They then went out to the luncheon room. The Inspector asked, "This door was locked?" When this was confirmed, he pointed out the key hanging on its hook in the right-hand door frame saying, "Not very secure, in the circumstances was it?"

Then seeing the unbarred open window at the end of the room, he asked, "Why isn't that window barred?" The Manager replied that it was some distance off the ground and as such access to the office through it was most unlikely. He also pointed out that the window opened outwards, and bars would be impractical.

The Inspector then interviewed the other staff individually. They were a very intimidated lot, scared stiff at being caught up in all of this. None admitted to any knowledge of the missing money, all saying they did not know it was in the lunchroom. Their body language gave no indication of guilt.

The alarm system was tested successfully.

The Inspector then asked to search the Manager and Accountant's cars. Search of the Manager's car revealed nothing. He came back inside for his 11:30 appointment.

When he approached the counter, he acknowledged the older lady standing there saying, "Hullo, Mrs. Delgoa, how can I help you?" (He had to speak up louder than normal, because he knew Mrs Delgoa was somewhat deaf and sometimes got confused.)

The old lady explained that some six weeks earlier she had bought a new padlock for her cupboard and apologised that she had forgotten to give him the second key. The Manager was non-plussed. He thanked her and said there really was no need as neither he nor his staff would ever need to get into her cupboard.

Looking at him quizzically she replied, "But you will need it for the money!"

The penny then dropped as Mrs. Delgoa, the office cleaner, explained, "I came in last night at my usual time of half past five and cleaned and dusted as I normally do. When I went into the luncheon room to clean it, I saw all that cash. I said to myself, I am sure they did not leave this out for me. So, before I left, I put it in my cleaning cupboard and put the padlock on."

The Manager took the key and asked Mrs Delgoa to sit down for a few minutes. He hurried excitedly to the back of the office where the cleaning cupboard was located. As he did so, the Inspector and Accountant came through the back door after searching the Accountant's car.

Telling them to accompany him, the Manager came to the cupboard, unlocked the padlock, and pulled back the latch to open the door.

Nothing!!!!!!! The disappointment hit him in the stomach and he bent over in pain. The Inspector and Accountant looked at him stupidly.

He told them the cleaner's story. The Inspector pushed past him and started to rummage through the cupboard. At the back in a plastic container, there were the bundles of notes – the fifties, twenties, and tens of the cash delivery. Handing them to the Manager the Inspector muttered, "You are bloody lucky! You just got out of gaol."

They returned to the Manager's office. Before doing so, however, the Manager went out into the customer area to where Mrs Delgoa was sitting. He came up to her, surprising her with a huge hug and saying over and over "Thank you so much. You have saved our lives. We thought it was stolen." Mrs Delgoa stiffened and breaking free of his embrace, she said rather coldly, "No, I would never do that. I would go to gaol and who then would look after my Pedro?" She walked out the door obviously miffed. The Manager shrugged and went into his office. The cash was duly verified by count and secured in the branch safe.

The Inspector telephoned Simon Sinclair who was happy to be let off the hook. He told the Inspector to instruct the Manager to report to him tomorrow morning in town. When he carpeted the Manager, he gave him the rounds of the kitchen as he was primarily responsible. He told him he and the Accountant would receive formal warnings of misconduct that carried automatic dismissal on issue of a third warning. They would also be barred for two years from receiving any promotion.

A couple of days later, the Manager shouted lunch for the Accountant and himself at a flash restaurant nearby where they toasted Mrs Delgoa and the fact that they weren't going to gaol.

The Manager had invited her and her husband Pedro but she, somewhat frostily, had declined. As she said to her husband afterwards, "I am still annoyed with them. I thought I was doing the right thing by putting the money in my cupboard, but that horrible Manager thought I was trying to steal it. Perhaps it would have been better if I had left it where it was."

On reflection, perhaps it would have!!!!!!!!!!

GRAHAM TEMPLETON

Another Silly Man - A Money Laundering Dupe

One of the problems facing criminal elements is how can they dispose of the proceeds of their illegal activities so that the suspicion of law enforcement agencies is not aroused. Once the funds have been laundered though, they can be freely used for legitimate purposes and obviously there is a lot of skulduggery involved in achieving this end.

The proceeds of gambling are not taxed, and some advantage is taken of this by obtaining cheques from bookmakers and clubs for bogus betting.

Another less utilised but effective approach is to persuade a rogue bank Manager to accept large cash deposits but not report them to the Government AUSTRAC agency specially established to counter money laundering.

In Sydney during the 1970s, there was a scurrilous street newspaper called the Kings Cross Whisper. It was notorious for its contents. One article that came under notice of the banking fraternity was, "How to rob a Bank with a ball-point pen." The article set out different lurid ways to compromise a Manager so he could be black-mailed and coerced into illegal activity such as assisting laundering and making fraudulent loans.

So far as the ABC was concerned, no instance of such activity came to notice at that time. However, the ploy certainly had relevance in the contemporary world for criminals looking to launder their ill-gotten gains.

In one case for the ABC Bank, Graham Templeton, the married Manager of one of its larger branches in the Eastern Suburbs of Sydney fell for the bait of a pretty woman. There were revealing photographs and he was persuaded to open a bank account in a fictitious name and allow large cash deposits without reporting them to the government AUSTRAC agency.

The people behind the scheme were Middle Eastern drug dealers, ruthless individuals who would stop at nothing to achieve their ends. It was not long before the Manager had to agree to another allied group joining the arrangement.

He was thrown a few crumbs, a new car, a holiday cruise with his wife and a couple of liaisons with the earlier woman.

With the large cash proceeds of drug sales deposited in the bank account but not reported to the authorities, the funds in non-cash form became freely available for whatever use sought by the dealers.

They spent lavishly on houses, cars, and luxury goods. They had to be careful though that they did not attract too much attention from neighbours who might get jealous and report their lifestyle to the Taxation Office. In that event, the whole arrangement would come unstuck. While they were living high on the hog, it seems that both groups supported organisations in Afghanistan, Libya and Iraq which almost certainly had terrorist connections.

Each month, substantial funds were remitted to the bank accounts of individuals living in Sydney with Arab names. These men were hawalas, members of an international network operating what might be described as an underground money transfer scheme. Such arrangements had the specific advantage that money transfers under this scheme bypass normal banking systems and thus evade scrutiny by Government watchdog agencies.

These men would not accept cash because it might be tainted and might lead to them coming under notice of authorities. A transfer from a Bank obviated such possibility.

Hawala arrangements are based on implicit trust and the extensive use of connections such as family relationships or regional affiliations. Unlike traditional banking, hawala makes minimal or often no use of any kind of negotiable instrument. Transfers of money take place based on verbal advice between members of a network.

If for example, an individual in Australia wishes to send $100,000 to a contact in Beirut, the amount is remitted by bank transfer to his local Hawala. He in turn requests the Beirut hawala in his network to effect payment to the payee and this is done. There are no direct transfer adjustments between them. However, if the Beirut Hawala is subsequently requested to pay $50,000 to a party in Malaysia or Indonesia, he can request the Sydney Hawala who owes him $100,000 to make the payment through the network's hawala in those places.

Each hawala maintains a running account of his position with others and over time balances his books with each hawala he is indebted to. Any breach of trust is rare as the consequences for the individual concerned would be undeniably violent.

The branch Manager was aware of the large turnover of funds in the accounts and the lavish personal spending. However, he was completely unaware of the implications of the large transfers to individuals with Arab names.

But he was becoming more and more apprehensive by the day. He was a worrier in the normal course and his constant reflection on the predicament he had got himself into, put his whole persona into turmoil. He shut himself in his office and rarely ventured outside. His senior staff wondered what had gone wrong.

The drug gangs never made their deposits through the teller but did so with the Manager in his office. He laundered this "black" cash by including it in the branch's treasury recording the addition as being a transfer from tellers. His staff did not suspect anything untoward.

When he decided he must pull out of the arrangements and told the principals he could no longer co-operate, they threatened to send the revealing photos to his wife. He was terrified and considered coming clean to the Bank and taking the consequences whatever, they might be. But he could not bring himself to do it. He was a nervous wreck. He could not sleep, could not eat. At dinner at night, he would pick at his food, rarely talking to his wife and then retire to his bedroom to lie on his bed worrying what was going to happen to him.

One weekday morning, he did not appear for breakfast ready for work. When his wife went into his room, he was lying paralysed on his bed. He had had a massive stroke. He was conscious but only his eyes, very distraught, moved. He could not talk but made only unintelligible sounds. His wife quickly called the ambulance to take him to hospital.

For the rest of his life, the poor man was a vegetable, unaware of who he was, unable to talk or feed himself. He did not recognise his wife. The drug people visited him in hospital and readily perceived that he was not a threat. They closed their accounts.

The drug rings were uncovered when one of the daughters was married and there was an over-the-top celebration and public display. It was the focus of the media and inevitably the Australian Tax Office decided to investigate. As soon as principals got wind of an investigation, they hot footed it overseas with bundles of $100 notes and heaps of gold jewellery packed in amongst clothing.

They had over the years previously set up a couple of luxurious bolt holes in Beirut. They were well set up and safe from any action by the Australian authorities.

The Bank never did find out about their Manager's aberrant behaviour. Fortunately, neither did his wife, who visited him regularly and who talked glowingly about him being such a good man until the day she died.

LES FERGUSON

A Man who had a Stroke of Luck

Les was the NSW Deputy State Manager. He had been in the job for four years and for most of that time he had been Acting State Manager in the absence of the then Manager who was suffering from debilitating chronic pancreatitis. In the end, the Bank became impatient with his long absences, and he was told to retire.

Les had performed well amply demonstrating his ability as a lender in all its forms and as an able administrator. State business had also increased strongly under his direction. He knew he had done well and held high hopes of being appointed as the new man. He underestimated, however, the obsessive ambitions of Simon Sinclair, the State Manager for Victoria.

Simon was an impressive individual, tall with a good head of silver hair with a trimmed moustache to match. He dressed impeccably and had the gift of the gab. He was a very confident person and pushed himself at every opportunity, inveigling himself into every situation that would enhance his promotional prospects.

With his eye on the NSW job, he had gone out of his way to cultivate the Deputy Chairman of the Bank's board who lived in Melbourne. This hard-nosed individual was also Chairman of a large national rural services company. He carried a lot of clout.

Simon made every effort to attend all up-market social functions where he thought the Deputy Chairman might attend (like the Friends of the Victorian Art Gallery, Children's' Hospital fund raisers). He joined the same prestigious golf club and got elected to the Club Committee. He was always prominent in photos of members appearing in the Club magazine. He joined the same church.

When the NSW Manager's job became vacant, Simon approached him and gained his support for appointment. When the panel of potential appointees was submitted to top management, the Managing Director favoured Les Ferguson's appointment. However, the decision was one for the Board.

At the Board meeting, management's recommendation for Les Ferguson was overturned at the behest of the Deputy Chairman. Simon got the nod. In speaking in support of Simon, he said he had been most impressed by his ability to move in high circles and be a strong representative for the Bank. The fact that Les would run rings around Simon in day-to-day banking expertise did not come into consideration.

Les did not take the rejection kindly. He was cordial with Simon when he took up duty but quickly came to the realisation that he was a decided lightweight. He lost respect for him when within a couple of weeks of arriving he made serious errors when assessing large corporate lending proposals. Despite all his bluster, Simon did not possess the lending nous required at this level.

Fortunately, Les picked up the oversights and included appropriate comment to cover them before the proposals were submitted to the Credit Committee of the Board. He saved Simon's bacon but did not get any thanks.

Simon offloaded whatever onerous responsibilities he could onto him.

There was, at that time in the Bank, a culture of heavy drinking, particularly among the upper echelons. There were frequent luncheons for clients where alcohol flowed freely and heavy drinking sessions most afternoons after work.

When he was not attending University, Flite would drive Les home to Strathfield. Otherwise, Les would catch a cab.

Les' marriage was not good. Jean, his wife had kicked him out of the marital bed years ago on account of his drunkenness and snoring. They had not been intimate for years but some affection remained.

Neither wished to endure the trauma of divorce and financial squabbling and were content to live together and enjoy the good life such as they had. Neither had gone off looking for other partners.

Les was coming home more drunk every day as the weeks went by, fuelled by his resentment at Simon's appointment. His wife, sick of it, told him bluntly one evening that he was going to kill himself unless he stopped. He did, but too quick for his body to adapt. Three days later on the following Saturday afternoon watching the football on TV, he had a serious stroke. His wife noticed immediately and called an ambulance. He was in hospital receiving treatment within the hour. Thanks to her quick reaction, the impact was greatly lessened, and it was said that he would be OK without any lasting problems.

Flite went to see him in hospital. He had talked intelligently although with some slurring about his stroke, the way he was being treated and (vaguely) the bank. Nothing seemed untoward. After half an hour Flite thought it best to take his leave. As he got up to go, Les said to him, "Mate, where do I know you from in the Bank?" Flite explained that Les' office was the one next to his. Les just looked wry. It was a worry. But there was no need. Within a month, Les was back in the chair.

He had changed though. He rarely spoke or laughed. He no longer drank. He never ever queried staff and simply went along with their recommendations. Previously, he would regularly walk into Flite's office next door and come in for a yarn. Now he never did. When it was time for lunch, he would get up and have coffee and a sandwich in the coffee shop downstairs alone. He always declined Simon's invitations to clients' luncheons and never attended any staff social functions.

Flite was surprised then one day when at 11:30am, Les poked his head around the door of his office to say he needed to get out and go for a walk. He said he was going up to the Botanic Gardens about ten minutes away and he might be gone for a while. He wanted to clear his head. Flite asked if he would like him to come with him but Les shook his head.

He did not return to work.

Flite rang his wife that evening. He had not come home. He contacted Sydney and St Vincent's Hospitals. He was not there. He had not come to the notice of the Police. He had disappeared. When he had not turned up after two days, his wife reported him missing.

When Les left the office, he started to walk up to the Gardens but so engrossed was he in his thoughts about himself, he passed them. When he looked up, he was in the vast open area of the Sydney Domain grassed area. He kept on walking down into Woolloomooloo. He came to the two pubs on separate corners opposite one another, The Bells, and the Macquarie Arms across the road from the big disused Fig Pier.

He went into the Bells and started drinking. He sat there drinking alone, one beer after another until 6:30pm when the publican threw him out. He was seriously inebriated and befuddled. He did not have enough money for a cab home. He wandered stumbling and falling a couple of times. His wife, at home, did not enter his mind.

He lay down in a shop front and passed out. He woke at daybreak, urinated against the front door, and set off wandering the streets again. He walked up towards the city and sat on a bus stop seat to rest. He had not thought of going home or returning to work.

A homeless man passed him and seeing the state he was in, sat down beside him. Introducing himself as Paddy, he said to Les "You're new at this mate, aren't you? Haven't seen you around before." When Les agreed that was the case, Paddy suggested he best stick with him while he showed him the ropes. So, for the next couple of months Paddy and Les wandered the streets together, cadging food where they could and doing a little bit of begging to get some money.

Les was still wearing his business suit but without his shirt. His jacket was filthy. He looked terrible, even Paddy was put out walking with him. He said to Les "Mate, you can't get around wearing that bloody suit jacket" and gave him an old South Sydney football jumper to wear in its place.

Finding a secure sleeping place was always a concern. They were never early enough in line to gain access to the Matthew Talbot hostel for homeless men down at Central Station and get a clean bed for the night. They kept away from the nearby Belmont Park that Paddy said was full of blokes on drugs and very violent.

Paddy took him down to St Canice's church at the bottom of the hill from Kings Cross where several homeless people bunked down on its porch every night. There was safety in numbers. He also showed him where you could sleep undisturbed in small places between buildings, under bushes in gardens not frequented by people at night. They ate irregularly. Whenever they were able to beg some money, they bought and drank a flagon of cheap port or sherry.

Police and people from the Salvation Army and Vinnies had asked around trying to locate Les. The homeless, however, kept things to themselves and would not give-up any of their own (unless of course that person was violent and a menace to them all. Les was not.) He just became one of the many who just disappear without trace.

His wife did not mourn. She just took up with her boss, rented the house to an affluent Asian family and lived the good life from then on. They had no kids, so there were no repercussions from that end.

Les settled into the precarious existence of life on the streets. There were opportunities to reveal himself and seek help, but he preferred life as it was. They stuck together for a while until one day Paddy was arrested attempting to shoplift wine at a bottle shop. Les never saw him again.

One night, Les found a nice spot to sleep out of the rain in a doorway of a vacant shop a couple of streets away from the Bells and Macquarie Arms hotels. There were a couple of broken-down cardboard cartons already there that would provide a softer place to lie on than the bare concrete. It was a quiet area with little traffic and few passers-by.

He had just started to doze off under his blue plastic tarpaulin when he was kicked heavily in the head a couple of times and told to piss off. He was sleeping in someone else's spot. Possession in the Law of the Streets was by right of physical might.

His assailant was big and nasty looking. Les did not argue, got to his feet and groggily staggered away. He sat down in another shop front a couple of hundred yards away. His head was starting to ache badly, and he was feeling wobbly.

At daybreak, he started to walk the streets but was feeling extremely weak and unwell. His headache was getting worse. He was walking along a street of small, single level terraces. The pain in his head was excruciating and he was having difficulty standing. He leaned against the front gate of a small well-kept home. The front door was open but behind the intervening screen door was a big German shepherd dog that started barking furiously.

A woman came to the door and half screamed "Mein Gott, Otto ist das wirklich du?" (My God, Otto is that you?) He nodded in pain, and she ran to help him inside. She laid him on the bed and looked at him. "Wor warst du? Es warst so lange?" (Where have you been? It has been so long!") She mistakenly believed Les was her German merchant seaman husband who had gone to sea six years ago but had never returned. She had never received any communication from him and had always hoped against hope that he would return.

Anna Schumaker was a presentable 53-year-old, a trained nurse who worked at the Sydney Eye Hospital a few streets away. She quickly recognised that Les was extremely ill. In halting slurred German, he told her his head was aching terribly. The corner of his mouth was down, and he could not raise his arms.

"Otto" was having a stroke and she rang for an ambulance.

He smelled badly so she quickly stripped him and washed him with sandalwood soap and hot water. Then she dressed him in Otto's pyjamas. Anna accompanied him in the ambulance to St Vincent's Hospital in Darlinghust 10 minutes away. He was registered as a patient in the name of Otto Schumaker, aged 60. Born in Bremerhaven, Germany, Australian citizen. Occupation Merchant Seaman, Resident 27 Ernest Street, Woolloomooloo.

Examining Les now Otto, the doctor found two huge bruises on his head. X rays showed the cranial cap had a slight crack and that his brain was bleeding.

They also showed that he had suffered a recent stroke which obviously had not helped his situation. The doctor explained to Anna that traumatic brain injury causing the brain to bleed, frequently resulted in stroke with accompanying memory loss, speech slurring and intellectual impairment. They had been quick to start treatment, and this helped but they would just have to wait and see how he recovered.

Anna went home and prayed firstly giving thanks to God for returning her husband and secondly for his recovery. She was overjoyed that Otto had come back to her. She loved him still and visited him every day in hospital. His head was bandaged where they had operated to release the pressure on his brain. When they shaved his head prior to the operation, they had also shaved off his beard growth. Looking at him, this was the first time that Anna had seen Otto without a goatee and moustache. She liked him better like this. This person had Otto's light colouring and those very pale blue eyes that betrayed his north European heritage. Yes, it was Otto allright.

The man in the bed's German speech was slurred but he told her, somewhat haltingly, that he had no memory of his past. He held her hand and apologising, said he was sorry he did not know her but looking at her, he was glad she was his wife. After ten days in hospital, she brought him home. He was a bit slow mentally and when he spoke (in German), he spoke slowly, searching for the words.

(Les' appearance and German speech derived from his maternal grand-parents who had fled their German homeland in the early 1900s and emigrated to Australia after their parents had forbidden them to marry.

Les' father was an interstate truck driver and due to his long absences from home, the family lived with the German grand parents on their vineyard in Pokolbin in the heart of the famed Hunter Valley wine region. His mother and her parents spoke German in the house and understandably Les became fluent. Over the forty years since he had left home, he had rarely had occasion to use his German and his present hesitancy reflected this lack of usage.)

Anna returned to work at the Eye Hospital and left him sitting in the sun in her backyard. When she returned home, she was astonished. The dishes from last evening's dinner and the morning's breakfast had been washed and put away, the bed made, and the house vacuumed. Everything was like a new pin. As soon as she sat down, he poured her a schnapps and produced a smoked salmon snack.

She was ecstatic. The old Otto was a rough sometimes violent man who never lifted a finger so far as housework was concerned or anything else for that matter. This was wonderful. But it got better.

When she took him to bed, he was not the rough sometimes cruel lover that was the old Otto totally disregarding her needs. This new man was soft and gentle and coaxed her along slowly bringing her to a wonderful exhilarating climax. His Schwanz was bigger than she remembered too but she was not complaining. She prayed, thanking her God for his wonderful changed return.

Les settled into his new life, intuitively cooking, cleaning, and maintaining things as he had been taught by his industrious grand parents. He was happy and contented without any concerns. His German improved and he was convinced in his own mind that he was Otto Schumaker. He never recalled his parents, grand parents, wife nor the people he had worked with. In his mind, it was Divine Providence or some quirk of memory that led him back to his home.

Now that Otto had returned, Anna was able to successfully claim on his behalf the not insignificant proceeds of his savings passbook account and superannuation. She got herself a new kitchen and bathroom that she always wanted and replaced her old Beetle VW.

Anna had never been happier. She could not ask for more after all the loneliness and heartbreak she had endured.

God continued to be good to them both as they loved and lived together happily for the rest of their lives never realising that it was all a case of mistaken identity.

The real Otto never re-appeared to upset the apple cart.

A MAN WHO HAD IT COMING

Pride Before a Fall

One Friday afternoon prior to a public holiday weekend, work activity in the NSW office had slowed. Most staff having enjoyed a long liquid lunch were drowsily poring over files trying to make out they were working and wishing the clock to departure time.

Flite had been held up attending afternoon tea in the executive suite and running late he hurriedly left his office. Just outside, however, there was a well-dressed Asian man standing somewhat bewildered and obviously needing help. The executive reception desk was vacant and the visitor had wandered into the area without being intercepted.

When Flite asked whether he could help, the man replied that he wished to open an account.

Wondering why the visitor had not done this at one of the nearby branches, Flite ushered him into his office and rang through to the kitchen for some coffee and sandwiches.

Flite started to seek personal details and was subsequently gob smacked when his visitor produced a bank draft for $2.5million US dollars with which to start off the account.

The visitor, a Mr. Lee, was a senior member of an affluent Singapore based family group with wide ranging financial interests including apart from a large commodity trading arm, tin mining and rubber operations in Malaysia as well as a fishing fleet operating out of the Philippines.

The family was currently acquiring hotel interests and already owned prestigious hotels in Hong Kong, Kuala Lumpur, and Singapore. He mentioned that the family was currently negotiating for the purchase of an Australia–wide hotel/motel chain and was looking for a line of credit to assist with this purchase.

At this stage Flite realized he was dealing with a “big fish”. He excused himself and went down the corridor to the State Manager’s office to acquaint him with this unexpected business windfall.

Simon at this moment was napping on the divan in his office and was most annoyed when Flite, over the protests of the private secretary, woke him up.

When he finally came down and met Mr. Lee, he was his usual smarmy self. When Lee raised the question of a line of credit of $150 million he agreed without hesitation, giving Flite the job of finalizing arrangements with Lee’s people. Approval of $150 million was outside Simon’s authority and should have been submitted to the Credit Committee of the Board for approval.

When Lee left, Flite asked whether he should draft a note to the Credit Committee of the Board outlining details. Simon however, made it clear that he would look after it.

The deal went ahead, the only security being a letter from the parent group’s board confirming that the assets of the hotel chain would not be pledged without consultation with the Bank. Although flimsy, this “negative pledge” was not uncommon where the Bank was dealing with big undoubted companies.

Enquiries of several Asian agent banks, in fact, confirmed that the Lee Family Group had assets of some 25 billion US dollars and were very sound. Individual board members were well and favourably known and free from any scandal.

Nine months later, he returned, marching straight into Simon's office. He asked for another $150 million and got it. Again, the security consisted of a letter of negative pledge. Simon again declined Flite's offer to draft a brief note to the Credit Committee of the Board.

Some six months later out of the blue, Simon and Flite were shocked when it was reported in the financial press that a senior member of the Lee family had embezzled some $300 million from one of the largest trading entities in Asia, as rumour had it, a front organisation for the Chinese Communist Government.

Simon was deeply disturbed by the news. He was obviously very worried and developed a nervous tic that he could not suppress.

They awaited a reassuring call from Lee, but it was not forthcoming. He could not be contacted, and it seemed he had returned to Singapore.

One evening soon afterwards, Flite had come back to the office about 8pm, after attending university to finish off some work and pick up his car. He had just settled down when he heard some strange noises down the corridor. He thought he was alone, so he got up to investigate. When he got down the corridor, he could see some light under Simon's door and then the sobbing noise again. He knocked and went in! He was shocked by what he saw.

The office was a mess and smelled of vomit. Worse still, there was Simon with his shoes off blubbering like a baby and unsuccessfully attempting to clamber up on to the windowsill to an open window. The office was on the nineteenth floor.

Flite grabbed him and pulled him away saying "What the bloody hell do you think you are doing?" He blubbered back saying "I have done my career, done everything! It's all over!" It then came out that he had not told the Credit Committee and now that, as he saw it, the Bank was almost certainly facing an immense loss, he was finished and could not live with the shame!

Flite sat him down and tried to calm him. He pointed out that the embezzlement was overseas not directly connected with their arrangements. In any case the group were very sound and almost assuredly could negotiate a satisfactory settlement for the fraud debt. It did not go down well. Simon was feeling too sorry for himself!

Flite put Simon's shoes on and called up his driver who was waiting patiently in the building's car park basement. The pair of them got him down into the car. Flite then rang Simon's wife to say he was on his way home and that she should put him straight to bed as he had had a bad day. Flite cleaned up the office as best he could and left a note for the contract cleaners who came in at 6:30am.

Simon did not front the next day. On the following day, he deputed the new Deputy State Manager, Max Kuhn (formerly the Group Leader, Western Division) to report matters to the Board's Credit Committee. He did not have the intestinal fortitude to front himself.

As it happened the Credit Committee just took it in. A couple of the members knew Lee from his racing connections (he owned a couple of racehorses and was, as they were, a member of the prestigious Australian Jockey Club). This was the focus of discussion. They accepted that the Group was strong asset-wise, would not want to see their business reputation or family honour tarnished and that the chance of any adverse impact affecting the ABC Bank was remote. The minutes simply noted the approval.

Simon never mentioned the incident to Flite nor did he offer any thanks. Probably it was unlikely that he would have jumped because, apart from anything else, he could not physically get up on to the windowsill.

As Flite and the Credit Committee surmised over the next few months the Lee Group negotiated a satisfactory settlement with the major entity without unduly affecting their overall financial situation. The ABC Bank deal never missed a beat and progressed to a satisfactory conclusion.

Simon never really recovered his former poise and confidence. He spent the next 6 months keeping the seat warm with little enthusiasm for his responsibilities.

He retired and he and his wife acquired a penthouse unit overlooking the beach on the Gold Coast and spent their days playing the one-armed bandits at the Tweed Heads Services Club. He died two years into retirement.

A MAN WHO FELL UNEXPECTEDLY

It all started at Simon Sinclair's retirement farewell for NSW Admin staff. The party started at 5:30pm on the Friday he retired, in the Staff Luncheon Room on the Head Office premises in lower Macquarie Street down near the Quay.

The catering staff turned on a marvellous buffet and an open bar was operating. After the farewell formalities, there was a disc-jockey and the middle-aged married romeos were in fierce rivalry with the younger men to dance with the girls.

Erik Nielsen wasn't dancing and as he walked over to the bar for a coke, he noticed a young woman he had never seen before sitting by herself nearby. He wondered why she was not dancing. She was pretty and he was surprised she had not been knocked over in the rush to dance. He went over and introduced himself asking where she worked as he had never seen her around before. He was surprised when she responded first by telling him "I know who you are Erik. I see you often at the beach steering your surf boat." She then added "I am Heidi Gustafson, I work on the floor below you on the switchboard."

He then asked, "Why aren't you dancing?" She blushed and a bit embarrassed, murmured, "I can't Erik. I have cerebral palsy and a gammy leg. I just can't." Erik apologised and then asked, "Would you like to dance with me?" She looked at him frowning and until Erik said, "Come on then my beautiful Heidi, put your arms around my neck" and picking her up and cradling her, he carried her to where people were dancing. He waltzed around the floor for a while and then stood swaying with her in his arms to the music.

Therese Briden, was sitting talking to a couple of the Divisional Group Leaders. Alcohol had been flowing freely and its influence was beginning to show. Some were already tipsy and she was keeping her eye on proceedings to make sure people, particularly the older men dancing with the young girls, were behaving.

Although a toughie, Therese did have a human side. She was also very perceptive. Noticing Erik and Heidi, clinging close, oblivious to those around them, she thought to herself "That is starting to look serious!" Then, in a moment of sheer inspiration she turned to the disc jockey and said, "Play that romantic Johnny Mathis' version of 'Moon River'".

The pair cuddled even closer. When Moon River concluded, Erik carried Heidi back to the table. They spontaneously hugged and then kissed in a lingering embrace. Therese smiled. There WAS a romance in the making. Heidi already had a secret fancy for Erik but for him, it was all new as this wonderful feeling of tenderness towards Heidi swept over him. It happened just like that.

A surf club mate who drove a taxi at night picked them up and dropped them at Heidi's place on Ramsgate Avenue halfway out from North Bondi beach to the Ben Buckler headland. When they arrived, he saw it was in a great spot, right on the cliff edge overlooking the beach. The unit was on the ground floor. She explained that she regularly looked out to watch him from the balcony but did not tell him of her daydreams of being with him.

When they arrived at her front door, Erik insisted he meet her mother. (She had already told him that her father, a senior police officer had been killed in the line of duty).

Her mother, Elsa, an older version of Heidi with a blonde plait, was a primary school teacher at the nearby North Bondi public school.

Erik explained to Elsa that he would like to see more of Heidi, if she were agreeable, and bearing mind that Heidi was special, he wanted her mother to see what sort of a man he was and to assure her he would look after her.

Elsa was impressed by Erik and his thoughtfulness in approaching her. She readily gave him her blessing.

Heidi took him to the front door and as he held her and kissed her lightly on the lips, he said, "You are beautiful, Heidi!" Then he jogged home along Hastings Parade, turned into Wairoa Avenue and then into Blair Street where he lived. He went to bed, shaking his head, muttering, "I think I am in love!"

On their first date, he took Heidi to dinner at the up-market Bondi Icebergs restaurant (the name deriving from a group who swam every Sunday morning in winter in the adjacent Bondi Baths). Heidi was wearing a lime green silk Vietnamese ao dai, a long top with a mandarin collar with splits either side and long pants of the same colour. She looked beautiful.

Erik was entranced. He, of course, was well known in the Bondi Beach community. As luck would have it, there was a party of surf club people also dining at the Icebergs that night.

As he and Heidi entered the restaurant there was an immediate clamour from that table.

"OK Viking! Where have you been hiding her?"

"Bloody hell, Viking, you are punching above your weight there!"

When he introduced Heidi to his surf club mates and their partners, she was given a lot of friendly, ribald advice and told things she did not know about Erik.

But she handled it well. When they called, "Watch him Love, he is a wild bugger!" She responded, (much to Erik's delight) with "That's why I love him." Which brought a long "Ooooo" from the table.

When one of them called "But you can't have known him long?" she replied, "You wouldn't know, of course, but I have known him and fancied him for a long, long time." Which resulted in another long "Oooooo" from the table.

Which, as she explained later at their table, was very true in the light of their time in the Bank together and her long-time daydreams about him.

They enjoyed the meal and one another's company. Erik told her of his childhood on a cane farm on the far north coast of New South Wales and his love of the surf. He explained that summer was normally a busy time for him with his surf club commitments but now he had met her, he would have to do something about that.

He mentioned that when he was in high school up the north coast, he was only a little bloke and initially was badly bullied. However, an old Chinese man who was the school's odd job man saw him being attacked one lunch time and intervened. He subsequently taught him the fighting techniques of the southern Chinese martial art of Wing Chun. He was able to look after himself very well from then on and the bullies left him alone. He told Heidi he continued with it and trained every day with his wooden Muk Yang Jong training dummy. She giggled and commented that that must look funny fighting with a wooden dummy. She asked, laughingly, "Do you ever win?"

Heidi talked about her father and what a great dad he had been. She and her mother had been devastated three years ago when her father had been shot by a drug crazed husband when responding to a domestic violence call.

She talked about her cerebral palsy and how it affected her .... her gammy right leg and sometimes stiff right arm but fortunately little else. She mentioned that she had had a couple of boyfriends in the past, but her disability had eventually turned them off. Erik touched her arm tenderly and said softly, "I am not going anywhere Heidi, if you want to be rid of me you are going to need a hard broom!" She giggled and muttered softly, "I don't have a hard broom and won't be buying one." Erik laughed and kissed her, which brought another long "Ooooo" from the surf club table.

He drove her home, took her to her front door and kissed her tenderly. As he left, he told her, "Heidi, you have cast a spell on me. You are very special." She smiled lovingly and said, "Erik, I have dreamed for a long time of being with you and now I am, I am so happy."

From then on, they regularly saw one another either going to dinner or to see a show. Often Erik would take her for a walk on the beach promenade in her wheelchair or they would sit side by side on the unit balcony holding hands and listening to the sounds of the surf below.

Their love deepened although they were never intimate. She was very fragile, and Erik was apprehensive that if he came on strong it might scare her off. He was always very tender with her.

One night after they had been to dinner and they pulled up outside her unit block, he leaned over to kiss her. She responded strongly and burst out tearfully, saying, " I love you Erik, I love you so much, I desperately hope you love me." He held her head and looking into her eyes, replied, "My Heidi, I am crazy about you, I have loved you since the moment we met, and I danced with you. I want you so much."

It was now October and surf carnivals were starting. But the following weekend after work on the Friday, they drove to the Lillianfels resort in the Blue Mountains. They had dinner in their room after which Heidi insisted, he take a shower. He came back to the bedroom wrapped in his robe and opened a bottle of chardonnay. He poured two glasses.

Heidi scurried off quickly into the bathroom. She was a while. When she emerged, she had her robe wrapped around her. She had blow-dried her short blond hair so that it was soft and fluffy. She came over to where he was sitting and Erik indicated that she should come sit beside him. He picked up a glass of wine and offered it to her.

She shook her head and then standing a few feet away let the robe slip off her shoulders. She stood there naked in front of him, her arms held slightly away from her sides with palms turned outwards. She stood there obviously very nervous and in a small voice asked, “Am I all right? Do you like me?”

Erik stared entranced for a full minute as he enjoyed the sight of her. She was beautiful, a positive delight, pert and very desirable. If there were any imperfection, he did not see it.

He jumped up off the divan, letting his own robe fall off his shoulders. Then naked, he picked up in his arms and carried her to the bed. Over the moon, he told her how gorgeous she was and how lucky he was to have met her. She started to cry saying she had been so frightened he would not find her attractive.

He laughed, telling her “I love you Heidi, I am crazy about you and I am going to marry you if you will have me!” She asked, “Do you really mean that?” He replied, “We have only known one another for a short while but I am certain in my mind that I want to spend the rest of my life with you.” She hugged him and said, “All my dreams have come true. I feel the same. I love you so much.”

They made love, Erik slowly and tenderly arousing her until she climaxed in a long paroxysm of joy as he did.

They had a wonderful weekend together and returned to Bondi on Sunday evening. Heidi was radiant as she hugged her mother. Elsa stood back and looked at them both with a big smile, “Obviously, you enjoyed one another’s company.” There was no doubt about it, but they did not tell Elsa about their commitment.

They took their annual holidays together at Easter and he took her to meet his parents at their farm in the country west of Ballina.

They welcomed Heidi warmly and his younger brother and wife who lived and worked on the farm teased Erik unmercifully about falling in love. They and his Mum and Dad never believed it would happen.

His Mum was particularly pleased that like her and her husband, Heidi was of Scandinavian stock and was familiar with their traditional customs. When Heidi entered the house, she laughingly pointed out the family Paskris, the feather Easter tree with the eggs hanging from it, that symbolised the end of the northern winter. To his mother's delight, Heidi closed her eyes and did the "fairy walk" three times around the tree making a wish she would not disclose (but we can guess).

Erik talked to the President of the Surf Club about his situation and received a sympathetic hearing. He stood down as Boat Captain and Sweep of the senior surf boat but remained an active member and continued to meet up with his mates. The club president and his wife were very impressed with Heidi when they invited the pair for dinner at their Rose Bay home. He later told Erik "You are a very lucky man indeed."

At Christmas, they announced their engagement with Erik producing a re-modelled ring of his paternal grandmother which incorporated a huge South African diamond his grandfather had acquired whilst working there as a mining engineer.

They planned to marry the following June.

Erik owned his two-bedroom unit in Blair Street after receiving a hefty inheritance from his paternal grandmother's will. When Erik sought Elsa's blessing to marry Heidi, she had suggested that he might like to come and live with them rather than at his own unit. She knew Heidi would welcome that and that she had no objection to them sleeping together. She told Erik that without a man in the house she felt vulnerable for Heidi and herself particularly as many of the occupants of their unit block were renting single men some of them very rough looking. Whilst she and Heidi kept to themselves and had little contact, she felt there was some risk.

Erik jumped at the opportunity to be with Heidi and moved in shortly after with his wooden Muk Yang Jong training dummy much to the women's merriment. He rented his unit.

The arrangement worked well and harmoniously Elsa respecting their need for privacy.

One Sunday evening when they were having dinner together, the peace was rent by extremely loud rock music from the unit above them. It was very intrusive and so loud that they had difficulty hearing one another.

Elsa said it was the new tenant who had moved in during the past week. Erik got up from the table and went upstairs to the unit above. When he knocked on the door it was opened by a big tough looking man who ignored Erik's proffered hand and attempt to introduce himself. He gruffly asked, "What the f…k do you want?"

When Erik politely said, "Your music is loud mate, would you mind turning it down a notch or two, we can't hear ourselves speak!" The big man snorted and grunted, "Get stuffed!"

To which Erik replied, "Come on mate, do the neighbourly thing."

As he turned to leave, he sensed a blow coming and tried to step back. Nonetheless the big bloke's fist still crashed into the side of his face. Although momentarily stunned, his martial arts expertise intuitively kicked in.

He correctly "settled his opponent" by putting his left arm around his waist and drawing himself close. Then, he brought his right knee up hard into the groin. The big man let out an agonised half-scream and sagged at the knees. Erik settled him again by placing his arm on his left shoulder. Then, with the heel of his open right hand he smashed his nose with a violent upward movement. The claret flowed profusely.

The man staggered back to the wall and slid down to a sitting position. Erik left him there. Fifteen minutes later the music was turned off.

At work on the following Wednesday, Arthur Smythe-Parker called on Erik to discuss those delinquent hard-core Southern Division loans that had been passed over to his firm for collection. When he saw Erik's badly bruised face, he asked how that had come about. After Erik explained, Arthur said, "He sounds like a bad bugger. I probably know him. Do you know his name?" When Erik said he didn't, Arthur said "No worries, I will check the bastard out!"

A few days later, Arthur contacted Erik and told him he was very lucky to have bested his neighbour, Paul Melek, who had a reputation as a very violent individual. He had been a bouncer at several Kings Cross clubs but had been sacked by them all due to his excessive aggressiveness.

He also owed money, over $20,000 to Sam Bitinsky, the owner of the illegal gambling club, "The Ace of Spades" notorious as the haunt of well-known criminals.

Arthur went on to say that he had been engaged by Sam to call on Melek and demand payment. If this were not forthcoming, he was to tell Melek he had 72 hours to come up with the cash before Sam would send his heavies.

Arthur was only a little man who dressed foppishly. He sported a line thin moustache. He certainly did not look formidable. When Melek answered his door, he had a bandage round his head with much padding around the nose. When he heard Arthur's message, he laughed and reached out to grab him saying, "I'll give you something to take back to that bastard Bitinsky."

As he did so, he was grabbed, one on each side, by two Pacific Islanders in black track suits with hoodies. They slammed him face forward against the wall. His nose started to bleed again through the bandage.

They turned him round to face Arthur.

Arthur repeated his message. When Melek spat at him, Arthur pinned a piece of paper on his chest saying "72 hours" took a polaroid photo and left.

The two Islander boys then gave him a going-over that caused a lot of pain but left no marks. They left him, dazed sitting against the wall outside his front door. As they left the building, they cut off his electricity in the meter box.

Arthur contacted Erik the next day saying, "Not surprisingly, Melek had done a runner late the previous evening but had run straight into the arms of Sam Bitinsky's men who were waiting for him."

He never returned to his unit and just disappeared. Nobody ever enquired as to his whereabouts.

Even though he had only lived there a short while, his unit had been trashed with half eaten piazzas and takeaway on the table and floor, empty bottles and syringes lying around, and furniture smashed.

The renting agent was sacked by the landlord who gave strict instructions to the new agent as to future tenants. The new people were an English couple with a young daughter who started at Elsa's school. With this association, both families became friendly and got on well together. Elsa, Erik and Heidi never again had any neighbour problems.

They married in June on the terrace of the newly renovated surf club building, the Surf Club President/Board Chairman proudly escorting a beautiful, radiant Heidi down the aisle and giving her away.

The guests apart from family were a mixed lot, a few from the bank, Flite and his wife, Erik's team leaders and their wives and a couple of Heidi's friends plus a big surf club contingent. But they all got on well. The formalities were brief, speeches short and ribald. The catering was wonderful, and everybody enjoyed themselves. As Erik and Heidi left the reception for their hotel, they passed through a guard of honour archway of crossed surf boat oars.

They honey-mooned in Japan. The cherry trees were still in bloom and the gardens were wonderful. Heidi thoroughly enjoyed it all. She was not capable of walking far so when they went shopping on the Ginza or they visited the tourist spots like Nara, the Heian Shrine and the Golden

Pavilion, Erik insisted she use her wheelchair. Where there were steps, he carried her.

He never tired of looking after her. Heidi in return loved him intensely, continually thanking God in her prayers for giving her this wonderful man of her dreams.

The highlight of their time in Japan was a lunch time visit to a traditional Japanese restaurant in the ancient capital of Kyoto. There they sat cross-legged on a wooden platform above a beautiful pool in which coloured Koi carp swam. Cherry trees in full bloom arched over the pool with multi flowering azaleas at their base.

There was a gentle waterfall and to add to this wonderful ambience, there was traditional soft koto string and flute music.

Erik and Heidi were entranced further when a young woman in geisha dress cooked shab shab, a hot pot of thinly sliced beef and vegetables in an iron pot at their table on a small coke stove.

It was truly a memorable experience. As Erik commented to Heidi, "This is so peaceful and serene, I guess heaven must be something like this." "In that case," he added, "I want to be there with you, so I better be good" and laughingly kissed her.

Nine months later, to their great joy, Elsa had a little girl. Heidi had got through her pregnancy well with no aftereffects. Two years later, she had another little girl.

With the added family, the Ramsgate Avenue unit became impractical. Elsa and Erik both sold up and bought a one level villa with a small but decent sized backyard in nearby Brighton Boulevard still close to the beach.

Erik and Heidi continued to live there as they grew older, still happy and devoted to one another. Erik remained an active Surf Club member and was heavily involved with the kids Nipper group, firstly with his own blond, blue-eyed daughters and in time, his grand kids.

Elsa lived to see both her granddaughters married on the surf club terrace and have children of their own.

And from time to time, Erik reflected on how it all started when he went to get a coke at Simon Sinclair's farewell. He certainly wasn't expecting to fall in love with his life partner minutes later!

In answer to Heidi's dreams, Lady Fortune, no doubt reinforced by Johnny Mathis, spun a web that ensnared them both.

It was a truly wonderful and unexpected outcome.

ROGUES, BLOODY ROGUES...

And then there are Bankers!

Source: Evan Jones (2019)
"The foreign currency loan experience in Australia"
www.bankvictims.com.au

As the 1980s approached, Australian Banks were still held back by quantitative controls and regulation originally enacted in the immediate post-war era. These arrangements had become increasingly out-dated and in 1981, the then Federal Government initiated a wide-ranging inquiry into the Banking System.

The recommendations of this Committee of Inquiry (Campbell Report 1981) sought extensive deregulation and privatisation, and these were gradually implemented by successive governments.

A concurrent concern to local banks was the granting of banking licences to foreign institutions who were expected to compete aggressively in their efforts to capture a worthwhile market share. Not surprisingly, the local banks reacted strongly and now freer from regulatory strictures, became increasingly more proactive with their lending.

One of their initiatives was to assertively promote borrowing in foreign currencies (mainly Swiss francs, Japanese yen and US dollars) to small business owners, farmers and property developers.

The major attraction (and selling point) with these loans was access to much lower interest rates (at the time 7.0% p.a. as against local rates then in the range 13 to sometimes 16% p.a.).

Prospective borrowers were led to believe that rates were stable and any adverse movement unlikely. Consistent with this assumption, the loans were unhedged, that is, there was no incorporated insurance to cover the risk of an adverse movement in exchange rates. The point at issue being that the cost of such cover would have obviated the lower interest advantage.

Another tool in common use in forex trading to protect either of the parties if exchange rates turn sour is a stop/loss mechanism. It does not seem that there was any consideration given to including such an order in loan arrangements.

There was little perception on either side of the wider ramifications, and it was a clear case of the blind leading the blind.

Soon afterwards in 1983, the Australian dollar floated, a development that opened the door wide to the inevitable debacle that followed. The scene was set, a classic scenario for "murphy's law," that is, "that if anything can go wrong, it will!" And it did!

Despite bank staffs' ill-advised assurances, in 1985 the newly floated Australian dollar fell significantly thereby bringing about a totally unexpected large increase in individual foreign currency borrowings.

Typically, someone with a foreign currency loan originally for $1,000,000 in Australian dollars found because of the unfavourable decline in rate differentials that their principal amount had doubled totally overcoming any interest rate advantage previously enjoyed. Borrowers' debt situations were further exacerbated by a plethora of excessive charges and fees.

Borrowers who could not come up with additional security for their increased debt and/or were unable to service it, fell into default.

There were thousands of such borrowers nationwide and Banks were now confronted with lending portfolios containing debts at risk totalling thousands of millions of dollars.

Huge write-offs were in prospect and in pub talk among bankies, there was even the wild rumour that one of the majors might "go to the wall." None did.

Then came the blame game with 15 years of bitter dogfighting. Borrowers with backs to the wall and scared of being ruined for life claimed Banks were at fault. Banks stood aloof taking their usual holier than thou stance. They countered that it was not they who were at fault but the borrowers themselves who had greedily pursued the lower interest rate and ignored the potential risk.

Resort to the courts brought little alleviation to borrowers with most judgments favouring the Banks. A few lucky people managed to negotiate a reasonable settlement but most lost everything.

It was thus inevitable that considerable opprobrium would attach to the Banks as a consequence. The facility was simply ill-suited for what it was intended. The Banks were not transparent and blinded by pursuit of profit and hopes of increasing market share, they were perceived to have been corrupt and rapacious.

Possibly, the most telling criticism was that of Justice Rogers who in a 1990 judgment summarised the deficiencies in the arrangement thus: "Nobody in his right mind, after being told that the possible loss was unlimited, that the necessary implementation of safeguards would be limited in their effect and would require continuous attention which the Bank refused to provide, would contemplate making the borrowing." (Evan Jones 2019)

A damming summation indeed!

The ABC Bank had been late into the game. Nonetheless it had some $800 million foreign currency high risk debts that threatened its survival in the short term if they eventuated in loss. The NSW component of this debt was some $550 million.

When other Banks entered the field, the ABC Bank had initially held off because of the perceived risk. Simon Sinclair, however, had seen it as an opportunity to gain some glory and had taken up the cudgels over opposition in his own ranks.

He made representations to the Bank's Board stressing that it was missing out on a golden opportunity. He had been given the "green light" and touted the facility strongly to his branch managers. The other states followed, all blithely following Simon blissfully ignoring the inherent risk.

By the time the disastrous ramifications of pursuing this line of lending eventuated, Simon had retired and gone to live on the Gold Coast.

The new State Manager NSW was the former State Manager for Queensland, a hard case but a shrewd operator and clear thinker. He set to in a very practical way to remedy matters, co-opting Flite and Erik Nielsen as a team to negotiate with borrowers to try and arrive at some mutually acceptable settlement.

They worked hard at the task but made little leeway. At the end of twelve months, the NSW State Manager had to report to Head Office that he could see no alternative other than to write off most of their recalcitrant loans. Other states were of same view.

This was the final blow for the Bank and the Board made representations to potential suitors. It was subsequently taken over by a Victorian based bank wishing to gain a greater foot hold in NSW and who prudently had little exposure to foreign currency loan risk.

Flite by this time, had obtained his master's degree in Forensic Accounting. When he was made redundant following the merger, he received a big payout. His wife was working as a high school teacher and earning good money. So, with his wife's blessing, he enrolled for his doctorate at the University of NSW's School of Business. When he graduated four years later, he became a lecturer and subsequently Associate Professor at the university teaching banking and finance. He enjoyed academic life and never regretted the forced ending to his banking days.

He and his wife were delighted when one of their twins represented Australia in the equestrian events at the 2000 Olympic Games in Sydney and won a silver medal.

He and Erik Nielsen and their wives remained lifelong friends. Erik was retained by the new bank and did well. He ultimately retired as Assistant State Manager for NSW.

The pair visited one another regularly and inevitably talked about their days at the ABC Bank. They occasionally referred to Norman and Simon and shook their heads about their antics and misdeeds.

They wondered about whatever happened to Les Ferguson. Flite invariably raised the tragedy of Timothy Flattery and the bloody mindedness that marred his life. It was so sad.

And so, the ABC Bank died. It was buried in a small niche in the National Archives, under "History of Australian Banking." It was not mourned.

There is no tombstone.

- The End -

CPSIA information can be obtained
at www.ICGtesting.com
Printed in the USA
LVHW081206021221
704874LV00022B/271

9 780645 283600